VAZEERI RUPI,

THE SILVER COUNTRY OF THE VAZEERS,

IN

KULU

VAZEERI RUPI,

THE SILVER COUNTRY OF THE VAZEERS, IN

KULU:

ITS BEAUTIES, ANTIQUITIES, AND SILVER MINES.

BY J. CALVERT, F. G. S., MEM. INST. C. E.

GYAN

Published by

GYAN

Gyan Publishing House
5, Ansari Road
Daryaganj, New Delhi-110002
Phone: 011-47034999, 9811692060
E-mail: books@gyanbooks.com

Distribution Network
gyanbooks.com
India, USA, Canada, UK, Australia, France

ISBN: 978-81-212-7951-2 (PB)
First Published, 1873

2nd Impression 2023

Printed at: Gyan Press, Delhi.

VAZEERI RUPI, THE SILVER COUNTRY OF THE VAZEERS, IN KULU
Author: J. CALVERT

Kell, Bros Lith.

GOING TO THE WEDDING_A LIKENESS.

KULU
AND
THE SILVER COUNTRY of the VAZEERS.

FARMHOUSE. KULU VALLEY.

London E. &F. N. Spon, 48. Charing Cross.

VAZEERI RUPI,

THE SILVER COUNTRY OF THE VAZEERS,

IN

KULU:

ITS BEAUTIES, ANTIQUITIES, AND SILVER MINES.

INCLUDING

A TRIP OVER THE LOWER HIMALAYAH RANGE AND GLACIERS.

With Illustrations.

By J. CALVERT, F.G.S., Mem. Inst. C.E.,

AUTHOR OF 'NOTES ON THE MINERAL WEALTH OF INDIA.'

LONDON:
E. & F. N. SPON, 48, CHARING CROSS.
NEW YORK:
446, BROOME STREET.
1873.

PREFACE.

THE outline of the present work originally appeared in 'The Englishman,' a weekly journal published in Calcutta, without the illustrations, and would have probably seen no further light than the *fire*, but for the flattering expressions of the Indian Press and the solicitations from persons of distinction for copies of the illustrations which accompanied the manuscript copy lent them. I am informed it was the perusal of this that induced Lord Mayo to alter his route and go through Kulu Valley, November, 1871.

When the late Sir R. Murchison asked me some years ago if I intended to publish the account of my travels in Africa, I replied that I did not think what I had *seen* would be sufficiently interesting. His remark was, "But there's great scope there for what you have *not* seen." Dr. Livingstone's book had not then appeared; but Gordon Cumming's *had*. My object in compiling this book has been as far as possible to describe by pen and pencil the beauties and interests of Kulu with *truth* if not with skill.

The nomenclature of places in India is perplexing

even to those familiar with the country and language. Thus one official calls it "Kooloo," which I prefer, but I have followed the Trigonometrical Survey Map, where it is marked as Kulu.

I had become somewhat acquainted with the mineral wealth of the Himalayahs when employed by Government some years ago to search for coal in Cashmere, but the Maharajah of Cashmere and the authorities of Chumba, also an adjoining independent State, discouraged the discovery of minerals, or virtually threw obstacles in the way of the mines being worked, the Resident of Chumba asking Rs. 40,000 to work an unopened lode.

The name of "Vazeeri Rupi" in British Kulu means "the silver country of the Vazeers," and the silver mines at Manikarn have long appeared in the maps. This excited my attention, and after some disputes about the right of search or prospecting, the Government very handsomely waived their claim to the mineral rights provided the Rajah would make terms, which with some difficulty was at last effected.

Government also granted a lease of the famous Shigri Mine, which has never yet been worked. The lode is antimony, from 15 to 20 feet wide of solid ore, capable of yielding 45*l.* per ton clear profit.

The mineral lodes in Vazeeri Rupi consist of silver-bearing lead, and copper lodes, and one or two of each were no doubt opened upon hundreds of years ago, but were built up and planted over to hide them from the Sikhs, and it has occupied over two years to trace out a few of the old workings and many more virgin lodes.

The Map is reduced from the Government Survey, with some trifling alterations and additions from actual survey.

The Illustrations, with one or two exceptions, are from my own pencil on the spot, the others from photographs by Bourne and Shephard, reproduced here by a special artist.

My thanks are especially due to T. D. Forsyth, Esq., for his encouragement at first, and to Col. Cox and other officials of the district for their support.

I am indebted also to Dr. Oldham, Chief Superintendent of the Geological Survey of India, and his assistants, for verifying my discoveries of the precious metals by chemical analysis, especially in the numerous lodes of silver-bearing lead.

These latter will form the richest mines that will be worked by the Company now forming.

From the time when Job declared "Surely there is a vein for the silver," and "The earth hath dust of gold," the same rocks bear the same treasures, the same labour gives the same result, and the same perseverance brings the like reward.

The late Sir Roderick Murchison assures us in his 'Siluria,' "that, looking to the world at large, the auriferous veinstones in the lower Silurian rocks contained the greatest quantity of gold," and that "though gold is the more restricted (in its native distribution) of the precious metals, argentiferous lead, on the contrary, expands so largely downwards into the bowels of the rocks as to lead us to believe that it must yield enormous quantities of silver for ages to come."

J. CALVERT.

KULU, PUNJAB.

OPINIONS OF THE PRESS

TO THE FIRST EDITION.

"In good time for the many who are now setting their houses in order and preparing for two months in the hills, comes Mr. Calvert's work on Kulu, its beauties, antiquities, and mineral riches. Mr. Calvert has already come before the public as the author of occasional papers on the mineral wealth of India, which have been published in 'The Englishman' and in this journal. He is well known to be an enthusiast with reference to the capabilities of the country still undeveloped, and has, we may say, devoted the remainder of his life to working out the problem which he advocates. Calm officials, without a care for the future, content to write their dockets and draw their salaries, gaze with astonishment on such men as Mr. Calvert. He is incomprehensible to them. They speak of him as an adventurer, and shake their heads doubtfully over him and his projects. In India the spirit that led our forefathers through the forests of the west, and the bush of the south, is sadly wanting, but we do occasionally find it here and there represented. We find a few persevering men settled in the lovely hill valleys fighting with red-tape obstructions, native passiveness, and extraordinary natural difficulties. In the higher valleys we find one or two men like Mr. Calvert fighting against the aforesaid red tape, still greater native stolidity and ignorance, and tenfold physical obstacles, yet confidently casting their lot there for good or evil. They may be ruined or perish, but the work of progress goes on; we are only slow to recognize the pioneers of its advance. What would Kangra have been were it not for the planters? In a few years we shall be able to say, what would Kulu have been were it not for the miners? But in spite of the general dreariness and sterility which is engendered in the strict slaves of routine, there is still enough of the old roving spirit in Anglo-Indians to drive them when on leave to break their trammels and betake themselves in a wild search for freedom to the mountain path, the glacier slide, or the jungle shade. Setting aside all commercial questions, Mr. Calvert's book on Kulu will be to that latter class a most acceptable contribution. But a few days ago we undertook to get for a friend bound for the hills information of the chief routes and works descriptive of the various hill districts. But after tapping every source we found we were still sadly deficient. We found that not a few travellers had written works on Cashmere all more or less excellent, but regarding the hills between Cashmere and Simla we found little or nothing. In another column, this very day, appears a letter from an officer wishing to know of these Kulu, Lahoul and Chumba routes, and we think it would be a public service if such travellers as he would send to the local papers accounts of the various stages of their journeys and the chief difficulties to be overcome. It is not so much general descriptions of the beauties of a locality that are wanted for travellers. Men travel as often as not to overcome difficulty and relieve the weary mind rather than simply to admire mountain scenery, and, at any rate, everyone can judge of the beauties for himself; but we want to know the length of stages, the provision required, the accommodation and labour attainable, the mountain difficulties, and relative advantages of rival routes. Mr. Calvert's work comes in good time to supplement our limited knowledge of Kulu. He describes with the utmost minuteness the routes to Sultanpore both from Simla, and from Jullundur *viâ* Kangra, giving the length of the stages, the description of the road, the places of interest to be looked at, the accommodation attainable. From Sultanpore he gives the same minute account of the routes over the Rohtang and Hamta passes. It is of course beyond the scope of a short article to give an idea of either the routes themselves or the scenes of interest through which they lie. Nor have we room for the enthusiastic description given of the untold wealth of ore and gems these almost inaccessible rocks contain. But the usefulness of the book is, we fancy, so apparent that no traveller will think of visiting Kulu without providing himself with a copy.

The author has a pleasing chatty style, he is full of local information, and is evidently of a very observing turn of mind. We trust he will succeed in the undertaking he has started, and we trust also that the light he throws on this little-known valley may be the means of opening up good roads to it, and encouraging and guiding future travellers."—'*The Indian Public Opinion and Panjab Times.*'

KULU:

ITS BEAUTIES, ANTIQUITIES, AND SILVER MINES.

EN easy "marches," or about 115 miles north of Simla—the celebrated and delightful Sanitarium of the privileged Indian Officials during the summer months—and in the same longitude, 77° 22′ East, is the capital and valley of Kulu or Kooloo, wherein are the sources of the "Blue Beas River" and its tributary sister the "Parbutti."

Kulu Valley is noted for much beautiful scenery which even Cashmere cannot equal, and for *variety* it certainly bears the palm.

There are several approaches or entrances to Kulu Valley, that by way of Kangra and the "Bubu Pass".

being the easiest as far as the road being wide and of gradual ascent, to which is added the convenience of rest-houses at every stage, those in Mundi territory being of a superior kind; but the British are almost always leaky, dirty, and badly attended. The Bubu Pass is over 10,000 feet high, and is impassable during four months every winter on account of the snow and ice, in which case the tourist must enter by the Bajara Pass, 7000 feet high. This is sometimes called "Tihir" Pass, from the village of that name on the Mundi side.

Moorcroft calls the river that runs down from the upper part to Bajara the "Ruperari," probably from the village of Ropur on its left side. This route is two marches longer than by the way of the "Bubu," and passes the Salt Mines and the city of Mundi; but there are no rest-houses between Jitringee, where the road turns off, and Bajara.

From the summit of this Bajara Pass is the first view of Kulu from Mundi boundary. At the end of the khud is seen Kot Kandi Mountain and the Temple and village of Dyar on the southern end. Behind this are immense forests of dark-leaved pines, which make a fine contrast in the winter to the snow-covered background of Giraub Mountain, 12,670 feet high.

There is another entrance from the south of the valley, and as it is often adopted by tourists from Simla on their way to Cashmere, and seems rather a favourite route, we propose to follow that, and point out the easiest way of visiting the most interesting spots and objects in the valley and adjacent country.

Starting from Simla by the route named in the Appendix at the end, and passing through some delightful scenery in the intermediate valleys, we reach Largi Rest-house, which is south of the "Saing" River and north of the "Chata;" we cross the river by a bridge, when it is not broken or carried away, by no means an unusual occurrence, in which case—without intending a pun — divers expedients are adopted to cross man and beast, which, though accompanied at times by some danger, but more fright, is seldom accompanied by worse results.

These wooden bridges are very picturesque, safe, and cheap; unlike bridges of masonry, or even iron, they can be built without the use of a boat or scaffolding, and even the abutments without mortar. The length of span which the principal timbers afford. at times 150 feet, and the height they are placed above the water, render them little liable to be injured by the timber and trees which are floated down the river during the occasional floods. The abutments, however, would be stronger if they were built at an angle of 45° to the stream, instead of at right angles, so as to turn off the huge masses of timber, which at times are carried down against them.

These bridges should be always hand-railed, but the incessant deflection of them, especially when cattle pass over, renders that puzzling to a native workman. A rope put through uprights would answer very well.

The boarding should also be nailed securely down, as I remember a friend of mine tilting one up and falling between the main beams, which supported his arms till I came to pull him up. With the few passengers usually passing he might, at another time, have had to practise his skill in gymnastics; but a man in that position, with his legs kicking about below the bridge, is rather a comical sight.

When over this bridge, called Largi Bridge, we are in "Vazeeri Rupi," the silver country of the Vazeers, part of Kulu. That mountain above is called Rungal, and is 9067 feet above the level of the sea at the top. If you were to climb up here you would probably see the quarry of precious serpentine, also called "verd antique," "ophite," "Moona Marble," &c., being very common off the Lizards in Cornwall. It is a silicate of magnesia, whence its medicinal properties, a lovely sea-green stone used for ornamental purposes, and according to tradition being eaten for liver complaint. The late Lord Mayo was anxious for me to get a piece for him, 4 feet by 2, to have turned and carved into a vase at Agra, where they are clever at that kind of work.

We will, however, continue the road, leaving the energetic proprietor of the quarry above to make his fortune by it.

BRIDGE OVER THE SAING RIVER FROM [illegible]ARGI TO KULU.

On turning the corner we find the "Blue Beas" to our left, and are entering the Kulu Valley. At present it has rather the appearance of a deep khud or ravine, but it soon opens on the view as we stop to light a cheroot under that pepul tree on the road. Below this some hundred feet is a spring of salt water, or "brine," that would supply all the country round with that necessary of life, salt. By the evaporation of this liquid in large open troughs or tanks, or by letting it run from a height over sprigs or bushes, the salt is precipitated and crystallized, and water evaporated, the result being table salt. Now we must move on, as Government will not allow that to be worked without a duty of Rs. 3 per maund, lest it should oppose the sale of their salt, of which the Government keep the monopoly — a policy we condemn in the Maharajah of Cashmere, but practise ourselves. The Rajah of Mundi has large salt quarries 30 miles from here, which supply all the valley, but pays no duty to the British Government, though it was lately proposed he should. It is expected the duty will be remitted off this, as the sale of it would only injure the sale of the Mundi salt, which is very impure stuff, and pays no duty to the British Government.

We must move on, as the next rest-house is 13 miles from Largi.

Now the valley begins to open, although this side is somewhat precipitous for a mile or two farther.

The other side is the territory of the Rajah of Mundi, and that high mountain on the left is Tong, 9060 feet high.

The Rajah of Mundi is an independent prince, if a prince can be called independent who pays Rs. 10,000 a year to the Government, and has the privilege of a British official residing with him, not only to watch all he does, but all he does *not* do. I can, however, personally attest to his urbanity and attention to everyone favouring his capital with a visit, and I expect he is indebted for his considerate thoughtfulness to his late tutor and councillor, Mr. Clarke, the loss of whose presence and advice he must much regret. But we shall have more to say of Mundi hereafter, which is but two easy stages from the next rest-house at Bajara.

This little village to the right is Dilasni, not so large a village, I expect, as it was 300 years ago, when the miners from the copper mines above used to bring all the copper here to smelt till that Devil "Choke Damp" frightened them all away. However, if you go up the adjoining khud you can pick up plenty of copper ore, which to the uninitiated shows itself in a lustrous green or a bright gold-coloured metallic crystal, that has, like a golden Eve, lured more than one man to ruin and starvation, imagining he had found gold. It is said that Major Hay reported gold in Kulu on finding a quantity of "iron pyrites," and it is certain he is not the last who made the fatal error. Gold may be always detected by this simple means,—it is malleable; no other yellow metal is so found but goes to powder when struck. Up above this khud, which exhibits the geological formation in a most interesting and distinct manner, is the village of Chisani, and above that numerous copper mines or indications, the green exudations from which show themselves for hundreds of yards, and bunches of ore have been worked out in many places to some little depth hundreds of years ago; the discovery of these old workings originated in finding pieces of ore in the khud below.

When these mines were worked the labour was compulsory, and was therefore thrown off the moment opportunity occurred, such as the incursion of antagonistic tribes, or may be the smelting was stopped for want of timber, which a few hundred years have amply made amends for now, or what is most probable, as with the Danes in Great Britain, the natives here never like to drive in farther than the sun shines, consequently the immense lode that can be traced for miles in the mountain above has been scarcely touched but in a few holes. These are called the Bilan Mines, being in the Bilan Kothi in Vazeeri Rupi, and have only lately been re-discovered. Specimens sent to the Exhibition at Lahore, 1863, are quoted as coming from "Bilan in Rupi."

There is no access to them up this khud, but there

is a path from Dilasni, and another from Badool farther on through the village of Chisani.

The green exudations can be seen from a great distance on the Mundi side opposite.

Come on. The road is wide and safe enough to canter, and the valley open to the left over the river, which soon becomes again deep below the road. Notice the limestone formation and those large blocks at the turning of the road just past this nullah. What fossils are these? a mass of oysters, or what? Break off some and send them to Dr. Oldham, and he'll put them on a shelf to bother some one else. Warington Smyth, Esq., kindly had a specimen I brought him cut and polished at Jermyn Street. He pronounced it *not* a fossil. The rock is composed of a mass of laminated formations about the size and shape of a breakfast-cup. One might fancy them a mass of petrified jelly-fish.

Go on, and the valley still widens; occasionally you will get a glimpse of the geological formation, which is very interesting if you bear in mind that the part below is limestone conglomerate, of pieces of a similar rock to that above.

That mountain to your right high above is "Jamere," 8973 feet, and I can say "beaucoup j'admire," for it is full of copper; but you can't get at it from this side.

Over the river, on the left, the mountains are thickly wooded, and, beside game, abound with wild

Kell, Bros. Lith.

FERRY MEN IN KULU WITH INFLATED BUFFALO SKINS.

hog. Above, on the right, you will see a stratum of fine limestone conglomerate lying unconformably on limestone shale, which dips at an angle of 45° S.

Now we come to the ferry below Badool village. The natives here adopt the method of lashing a charpoy on two inflated buffalo skins, and convey you and all your belongings over with the greatest ease, if not pleasantness. But be you careful while collecting specimens of that conglomerate limestone that overhangs the ferry, which is surpassingly interesting, if not unique, that some of those hundreds of monkeys that hang about above the projecting rock do not, by accident or design, roll stones down on your head or toes, or, swinging carelessly from a branch, *pukero* your topie or your wife's chignon, for such things have been done. It is not only cruel but dangerous to shoot them, or even pelt them, for they can, and do, retaliate, sometimes with fatal results. They are, however, the pests of the orchard and the cornfield, where they commit great devastation.

I was completely nonplussed when I sent some of the *red* rock from here to Calcutta to be assured it was "veritable bricks and mortar." I don't believe it yet.

Come now, get on the charpoy, call the dogs, and over we go. See how deep the blue water is, and so clear you can see the white sand and every stone below, and see the image of that monkey swinging from the tree above by his tail, the elasticity of his limbs enabling him to supply his daily wants without curtailing his gambols.

These monkeys may be seen about here and elsewhere in hundreds, some hugging their pretty little ones as if they really loved them.

Now we are in Mundi territory for a while, passing the village of Nagoad. The nullah from which this stream runs that we cross by this bridge leads to a fine shooting ground for pheasant, chikor, &c.: and they tell me, on those mountains are a peculiar deer like small oxen, but without horns. There are also large iron mines, which are worked by the Rajah of Mundi's people. The ore is iron sand.

At the farms up here some fine gram-fed sheep can be purchased at Rs. 8 each—sheep equal, I am told, to English.

We now ascend the road above one of the most beautiful turns in the Blue Beas, whose deep water below the road, cut in the precipitous and overhanging limestone rock, ever reflects that exquisite blue for which it is famous.

Descending to the banks of the Beas again many interesting stones may be *picked up*, though they don't pay to carry. The limestones here are peculiar in colour, and in some places impregnated with mineral, in which I found bismuth, a valuable metal, as well as manganese. This little rest-house at Thirri was built by the kind Rajah of Mundi for the use of travellers delayed by the floods from crossing the ferry. There is no charge for this shelter, but there is at all those we are coming to in British territory. In this consideration the Rajah of Mundi sets a noble example, compared to the accommodation and charges of our own Government, that needs copying. It is a disgrace to the Government to charge for some of the "cattle sheds" they call rest-houses in Kulu, to wit, Manali, Pulchan, and Rolla; there is no rest-house at Dobie.

If you examine the overhanging limestone rocks to the left of this rest-house, there is a small lode of bismuth and manganese ore in the pink limestone matrix, which will afford a very unusual cabinet specimen, although too small to work at a profit.

We must leave that and the black marble too, for here ends the limestone formation, and hasten on towards Bajara Rest-house, about two short miles. High up on the left is a quarry of white micaceous decomposed slate, which is quarried to use as whitewash, and lower down the hill the white beacons show the boundary of the Mundi territory, which we pass at this stone wall and are again in Kulu; to the left is the tea-house and remains of what was intended for a tea-plantation, but proved a failure in tea, though the tea-making house above is still used occasionally.

We now descend into the old bed of the Bajara Khud and wheel round to the rest-house, which forms a comfortable shelter, considering it is said to have been built for nothing, or next to it.

Take care of your dogs here, for I have seen a leopard attack a dog in the verandah during dinner time.

You must remain a day at least here, for you are in the widest if not the prettiest part of the valley. So see for yourself, or follow my descriptive guide.

There is a very nice walk for a mile or two up the khud here before breakfast, and you can even get a dip there under the rocks in a retired place, but never go without a stick at least, for some of the guddees, or shepherds' hill dogs, are sometimes in charge here over the flocks, and will boldly attack you; and some are so fierce, I have had to defend myself with my sword and kill, because I could not drive them off.

Some of these hill people reside during the winter in the caves excavated high up on the right—which hold not only families but *flocks* of sheep or goats—and return to their country during the summer months. These caves have, I expect, been dug out for some metallic mineral or the red clay that is found in this clayslate or sandstone shale formation. There are plenty of lodes of carbonate of iron in these hills, and some signs of lead.

There is an agent for the Tea Plantation Company resides at Bajara, who, if he fails in his tea, does not

Kell Bro^s lith.

ANCIENT FORT, BAJARA, AND TEA PLANTER'S HOUSE.

in his hospitality, where the generosity of the hostess is so amiably bestowed by the fair daughter; it would be impossible to omit the testimony which everyone bears to the kindness of the only European family resident at present in Kulu.

Here are the remains of the old fort of Bajara, which a horrid Vandalism has doomed to destruction for the sake of a few stones and rotten sticks of wood for fuel.

No doubt this interesting ruin of bygone days was much injured by the last siege of the Sikhs; but one would have thought anyone *purchasing it* would not have grudged a few rupees to have saved the only remaining fort of the kind in India from falling to decay.

It is probably the most perfect building of the kind extant, and should never have been sold by Government.

Centuries ago this fort must have bristled with the appurtenances of war, repelling the attacks of rapacious neighbours, or later still of such ruthless invaders as Runjeet Singh, who, it is said, at one time levied "black mail" on this place to the amount of two lacs of silver, the frail walls not being able to withstand his artillery, which

"Bellowed its deluge of immortal smash."

No doubt, however, many a native has there shown his great prowess in arms, fighting with sword in hand "for hearth and home," till made to "bite the dust."

No useless monument surmounts his grave, but for the sake of those who fought and bled, let the old stones stand.

In those days this fort no doubt gave good shelter to its defenders, till modern artillery brought by Runjeet Singh and the bold warrior Sikhs left no alternative but to submit, *and pay*.

Some parts of this fort must have been well constructed and well adorned, as will be seen by a stone used as a step to the tea agent's bungalow, not the only stone by many, I expect, used in the construction of this and other adjacent village buildings. The few that are left show no want of skill in workmanship or design in the rich carvings that cover them.

Not to be despised in either sense is an ancient "gurgoil," or water-spout, now used at the entrance of a Bunjah's store on the hill above the bridge, carved in solid mica schist. It forms an interesting specimen of carving and design worthy a modern sculptor, although reported to be more than 800 years old; whether this formed a "gurgoil" for carrying the water off a roof is perhaps dubious, though it follows many a similar design in English, and especially Norman cathedrals and other buildings in Europe; or whether it formed, as is more probable, the conduit from a spring or water-course where the early maiden drew her morning draught, or the more

GURGOIL, CARVED IN MICA SCHIST STONE
FROM OLD FORT BAJARA, KULU.

STONE CEILING, BAJARA TEMPLE.

CARVED STONE 17"×12", FROM BAJAURA TEMPLE KULU.

Page 18

J. Calvert

Kell Bros Lith London

tired traveller his refreshing bath, it is a very interesting relic of bygone ages in Kulu, and deserves a better position and protection than being thus "degraded, cast carelessly away."

Here no doubt dwelt the Negee, or chosen head man of the district or "Kohti," whose rights included certain authority over the unmarried daughters, as well as claim to certain "buckshees" and "dustoories," which increased the emulation for the important position.

But there are two other interesting memorials of antiquity, if not of superstition, close by. One is a temple and numerous detached carvings in the adjacent village. It was at one time reported there was a large amount of gold buried near this temple, and much digging ensued in search thereof, but with no avail, as may be supposed. It is impossible to say whether all the curiously carved stones originally formed one building, though now so scattered, or were part of some temple or building attached to the fort; they are well worth inspecting, although some of them are much mutilated and begrimed with filth. Most of the adjacent buildings seem to have been constructed out of stones belonging to some other building or temple.

The most perfect object, however, is a small temple of carved stone in an isolated spot to the east of the rest-house among the fields. This is comparatively perfect, considering it is supposed to be eight or nine hundred years old; the injuries to the carvings are not the result of time, but the wantonness of the Mahomedans, who from religious prejudice destroy all sculptured figures. Moorcroft relates (p. 169) that these sculptures were mutilated by the soldiers of the grandfather of Sandsar Chand when he invaded Kulu.

Bajara Temple is of a square plan inside.

The door and entrance porch is to the east side, and there are recesses on each of the three other sides in which are bas-reliefs. In the southern recess is the Elephant God, in the western the Goddess "Bowanne atpoojee" with her eight arms.

The figure to the north holds a long sword in her left hand, and a sort of rosette in her right; at her feet small devils are fighting.

On the entrance door jambs are figures whose legs are in plate armour; they have umbrellas over their heads, held in one instance by a small figure in armour; the other has more small devils fighting at her feet. They are all sadly defaced from mere wantonness.

The inscriptions on the door jambs *may* be more recent than the building, and merely note the visit of some person on pilgrimage who considered himself important; the style is like Sanscrit.

I have made a number of drawings of various carved stones in this temple, some of the figures being 4 feet high; and have copied some of the inscription,

DOORWAY BAJAURA TEMPLE.

DOORWAY BAJAURA TEMPLE.

BAS RELEIF, HEIGHT 5 FEET.

Page 16.

Calvert

Kell Bros Lith London

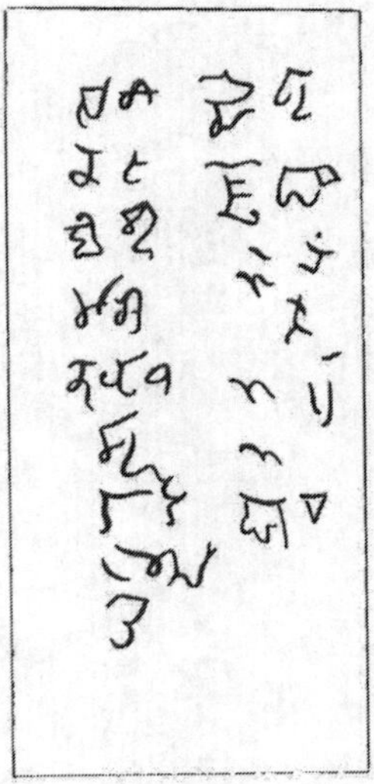

PART OF AN INSCRIPTION IN TEMPLE BAJARA KULU

Page 16.

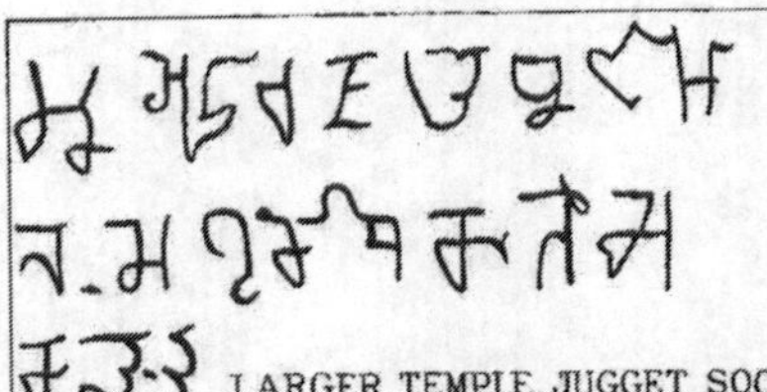

LARGER TEMPLE, JUGGET SOOKHT KULU

SUNK ORNAMENT BELOW BUNGALOW

Page 65.

Kell Bros Lith London

which no doubt can be deciphered by the learned; at least I remember Mr. Fergusson telling me at the Geological Society's meeting in London, that there were no inscriptions in India that could not be deciphered. This and similar buildings are constructed without mortar between the stones, but every stone has "dressed" faces, joints and "bed" fitting in its assigned place with great accuracy throughout—there being no "filling in" of rubbish so common with the P. W. Department, which evidently had no existence in those times. Nor were the architects who designed these enduring examples of their skill sent adrift on the world as unfit for further work at forty years of age, as in India now. No architect can earn a living in India, all buildings are designed by military men.*

The carving on one of the stones represents "Barachq," a figure half angel, half bird; I have seen similar effigies or figures beautifully executed in Delhi, at the Mohurrum festival.

It is related that "a French gentleman endeavoured to purchase this temple, with a view to having it removed;" but it would not be an impossibility to take casts of some of the carvings, though much defaced and covered with lichens.

Excepting the profiles of the three-faced Hindu triad, Brahma, Vishnu and Siva, which appears on

* See Fergusson's 'Architecture,' Section "India." Since this was written an Order in Council forbids the appointment of anyone above twenty-five years of age in the uncovenanted service.

each side, as also in front of the temple at Jugget Sookht, I have not seen similar carvings anywhere else. Whereas in Mundi territory and lower South, the temples are nearly all built after the same model.

At the Holy Lake in Riwalsir,* below Mundi city, I found some masons quarrying the rocks and building a temple very much like one I saw on the banks of the Beas below Nadoun. I inquired if the head mason had any drawing from which he executed the work; his reply was "No, we build on the same plan, and carve the same ornaments and designs as our fathers did before us; each man knows his duty and the work consigned to him:" a kind of practical Freemasonry that is said to have prevailed in Europe when the buildings, such as our early cathedrals, were erected, especially Salisbury Cathedral.

This temple has suffered much from lightning and earthquake, which has severed one section from the main building about six inches all the way down, the stones remaining, however, unbroken and still "toothed" into each other.

Hereon also "the mower whets his scythe," heedless of the execrations of the antiquary and archæologist, and thus wantonly defaces the most prominent stones.

The greatest injury, however, has been caused by lightning striking the iron rod fixed on the top. A

* These temples and the sacred lake of fish are probably a remnant of the fish-worship so prevalent throughout Syria, where temples and shrines were erected in honour of the fish goddess "Ducita."

ANCIENT TEMPLE AT BAJARA.

ANGELS ON STONE 17′× 12′, BARACHQ

OUTSIDE BAJARA TEMPLE.

CARVED STONE FROM BAJAURA FORT, KULU.

CARVED STONE OUTSIDE BAJAURA TEMPLE, KULU. 8×20.

Page 17.

J. Calvert

Kell Bro.s Lith London

severe earthquake is on record which occurred here not a great while since, and will account for this and other similar phenomena.

At Jugget Sookht Temple higher up the valley, the largest stone, three or four feet wide, has shifted about ten inches to the north, no other stone being displaced.

Sir H. De la Beche mentions similar occurrences, and I remember noticing the mullions of the windows of Kanturk Castle, Co. Cork, Ireland, have been turned a quarter of the way round without affecting the transoms or sills.

The altar inside is provided with gutters for the blood, but at present the sacrifices seem limited to some unfortunate mouse caught in the corn bin, or at other times of a few simple flowers from the field. At times, however, as we shall see hereafter, blood can flow freely enough.

There is a good view both up and down the valley from the adjacent high land.

The view to the east of Kot Kandi across the river is not without interest; the summit is about 7000 feet. But if seen from about a mile and a half up "Bajara Khud" it is better still, especially in the cold season, when the dark forests contrast so well with the more distant snowy heights of the Girault Mountain (12,070). On the right end of the ridge is the temple and village of Duyar above the limestone rock, which ceases here; below Kot Kandi are numerous large villages, and several rich lodes of copper, iron, and manganese, never yet worked; there is also good slate. The jungle and grass on this hill looks, of course, red and parched up in winter, but is beautifully green after the rains; there is, however, a great want of water on account of the geological strata dipping down in the opposite direction.

Looking across more southerly, is the Harla Khud, and on the other side of it the before-mentioned Jamere; there is a fair road up this khud, which abounds in copper ore from the Narole and other mines here; there are also fine white marble slabs or tiles in abundance from the limestone shales. This khud leads up to Kasal, 11,795, and is said to abound with game.

The Beas River is fordable in several places about here according to the season, offering facilities for crossing to the other side; during the heat and floods, however, some alteration takes place in the position where the ferrymen ply.

We will now leave Bajara, keeping on the road, as there is not much sport in the hills to the west, or left, unless you venture up to Kokan, 8520 feet, and its neighbouring forests, for pheasant and chikor. No shooting, however, is allowed here out of season.

Three miles from Bajara to the left of the road is a small hut temple under a tree, interesting so far only as being the deposit of numerous tombs or stones erected in memory of certain good and faithful wives who underwent Suttee with their beloved husbands' corpses years ago; there are many more at Nugger, but all are very inferior in execution to any carvings at the other temples like Bajara, which are of great merit both in artistic design as well as execution. Some of the scroll-work might do credit even in present days to a school of design; these, however, are apparently chopped out of sandstone by a village mason only, and usually represent the Rajah on horse, and as many figures below or above as were sacrificed at his death. There are no attempts at any inscription whatever.

Farther on is the village of Shumshee, which is so poor that there is no roof over the temple altar in the middle of the road.

In the river near here gold is washed for at certain seasons, but the abundance of large rocks in the bed prevents the sand being reached, and makes the success very small.

There is no doubt experienced gold-washers could obtain enough gold from this river to provide an ample living, but they ask too much for it when they get it,—never under Rs. 15 per tolah, impurities and all.

It is a certain fact that all the rivers in the Punjab, excepting the Ravee, produce gold; the Indus in particular.

"Twenty-seven kos. north of Sultanpur in Kulu, over the Chang Chinmo Pass, lies the Aksai chin, or, as the term implies, the great Chinese white desert or plain. It extends into Chinese Tartary. There are several lakes and gold mines in it. The gold mine of Ichidi, in the direction of Karia, one of the principal towns of Khotan, is one of the largest, where 1500 men (Khutanés) are constantly working for six months in the year,—June to November.

"Each man has to pay a tax of 1 'ser' or 3 tolahs of gold yearly for the Emperor of China.

"It is stated that the people in the mountainous districts to the north adopt the following ingenious method of collecting gold dust in the otherwise inaccessible precipices and ravines:—

"Previous to driving their flocks and herds of goats and sheep out to graze daily, they cover their feet with some gummy or other glutinous matter, especially between the hoofs, and on their being collected in the evening, wash it off every one; and from the dirt so collected they actually derive some little amount of gold dust collected from places where it is impossible for human foot to climb.

"These people, living on a little grain which their sheep carry for them in bags on their backs, and the milk of their herd for drink, traverse over vast mountainous regions of the Himalayahs unexplored by anyone else, and affording during the summer months sufficient pasturage to supply their flocks, while the lower lands are parched up, until the returning snow compels them to descend to the freshly-watered and more verdant plains.

"This gold is, no doubt, produced by the disintegration of auriferous veins in the rocks, which are for many months in the year subjected to heavy avalanches of snow and 'piteous storms'; and their little store of gold affords them some small ornament for the ears or noses of their females, or is kept as a last resource for time of want,—if such people ever can want, who find their meat, drink, and clothing provided for them by their flocks, and a home in the mountain cave."*

There is usually a ferry at work over the river about here.

Opposite here is the entrance to the Parbutti, which is reached by crossing at this ferry; and the high mountain to the north of it is Bijli, on the summit of which, 8070 feet high, is a temple to the goddess of lightning. It is easily accessible from Sultanpur by crossing the bridge there, and the view will amply repay for the trouble.

After passing along a pleasant avenue of trees, and following the river bank, we cross the Maol Khud; here immense blocks of copper lodes have been brought down from *somewhere* ages ago. Continuing along the river bed we begin to ascend with the road high above it, and after passing a spring of water under some large trees, the road is cut in the

* *Vide* 'Notes on the Mineral Wealth of India,' by John Calvert, F.G.S.

solid sandstone, and though precipitous and high above the river is quite safe.

From here may be seen the celebrated Sona-pani Glacier in Lahoul, and two mountains 21,000 and 22,000 feet high.

Nearer, and looking very picturesque, at the foot of the spur of the facing mountain, is Sultanpur, the present capital of Kulu, and a place of some commerce every autumn. It is also the residence of Rae Dhulep Singh, the present Rae, who is a minor son of the late Rae Jyan Singh, who died from an accident in 1870.

The Maidan south of the city has a fine appearance, and is kept free from buildings or cultivation for the especial convenience of the Devil Gods, Munders, Juggernauts, or Davis, of which it is said there are at least 150 in the valley, the lands with which they are endowed forming no inconsiderable portion of the gross area under cultivation.

They are maintained under the special protection of a benignant and liberal Christian Government, who will not permit a Christian to sacrifice his beef at Christmas, lest the Juggernauts should take offence!

Before reaching this, we pass Rile Khud to the left, where, high up, are large lodes of copper ore cropping out from the projecting rock.

Continuing the road, on each side of which are peach and apricot trees in abundance, we pass over

VIEW OF SULTANPUR, KULU.

the Maidan, and in the left out-of-the-way corner find the rest-house of Sultanpur.

Here, it is reported, you may "get anything," that is, provided you submit to the Assistant-Commissioner's prices, which are most exorbitant, at least were so in 1869–70. When the late Assistant-Commissioner was not residing the natives were more ready and willing to let us have all we wanted at moderate charges, although the tariff both for labour and provisions has been raised unnecessarily.

Opposite the rest-house is the Tehseel, near which is a small garden, "used to utilize the labour of the prisoners," by planting garlic and shucking peas for the Tehseel baboos. This was the official excuse given me for refusing to sell it me after it had been promised by the Assistant-Commissioner.

Those who have dogs must take care of them here, as leopards abound. I witnessed a fight between two on the hill at the back of the rest-house, which lasted for nearly twenty minutes, when they lost footing, and rolled down the mountain and separated.

At another time our party consisted of two ladies and two gentlemen; we had walked up the adjoining khud for more than a mile, and were close home, the dogs having hastened in advance for their evening meal, and the servants and weapons being all far in front except one dog, which we saw quite close above the road fighting with an old brown leopard, that I at first took for a small cow. The dog was on his hind legs, and evidently had hold of the leopard by the ear or lip. On our shouting out—for we could do nothing else—the leopard climbed up the mountain, and the dog, who seemed bereft of reason with fright, was found to have a longitudinal gash down his throat, no doubt caused by the leopard's claw. He lived, however, to be effectually chawed up the next fight.

Leopards commonly prowl about the city at night for dogs and *babies*; and it is not till the natives have lost a cow or calf, which they value more than a baby I believe, that they will combine to attack them.

The leopards, however, have a partiality for dogs, which are not safe in the verandah even at night.

Near the before-mentioned fruit garden will be seen a quantity of boulders placed in circles or kraals, apparently for the protection of cattle at night. Here was encamped the army of Runjeet Singh when he came to claim black mail, but it is evident they existed and in that form long before his time, as the lichens with which they are covered would attest, and might have been erected and used by the Lahoul people and others who seek this valley all the winter months, before there was accommodation in the bazaar to the north of the town as now.

The appearance of the surfaces of hundreds of the boulders here are a convincing proof that many thousand "curries" have been ground on them, and

THE DEVIL GOD IS TAKEN OUT WITH TRUMPETS AND SHAWMS.

many small round holes have been bored to serve the purpose of lamps.

There is, to the north of the rest-house, and at the corner of the road leading up the khud, a block of sandstone covered with a long inscription, which, could we decipher, might interest us much if not instruct. The round holes drilled in it are, I presume, to burn a wick in for light; probably it may tell of some great battle fought on that Maidan ages ago.

Twice a year the Maidan is covered with the Munders, or Devil Gods, who come from all parts of Kulu and the adjacent country for three days' fair or feast, and muster above a hundred, all accompanied by "tumtums," "trumpets, and shawms," some of which are of solid silver in the shape of the letter S joining in the middle, so that the mouth-piece end packs into the larger end when not in use; added to these is a species of "pibroch" with a cold, making, as Sydney Smith said of the St. Paul's organist, "a noise like a whipt whining cur."

Hour after hour this awful din continues until each god has paid his respects to the other village gods, and they separate into batches for the night in various parts of the Maidan.

The construction of the "Davi," or Devil God, in Kulu is in this way:—A kind of ornamental chair is supported on four men's shoulders by long bamboos; the chair is covered with rich silk or shawls, usually of red colour, with deep fringes of silver or gold, and where the back cushion is usually placed in our chairs are fixed from three to ten or more silver masks or faces of various sizes, according to the wealth of the village to which it belongs, and the value of its landed endowments; the masks have the eyes and features rudely painted on the silver, and do not do credit at all to the silversmiths of Kulu, who can turn out most excellent work, especially in the silver necklaces and tiaras for the women, and the blue enamel medals worn by almost every man.

Below this chair, it must be noted, is a large receptacle or bag, hid by the ornamental valance or hangings, in which the donations to the devil and the prog of the priests and followers are carried. This is capacious as Robin Hood's wallet, that held the Bishop of Hereford's "three hundred pounds." Nor must we forget the bottle with a "wee drop" of native "bang," made in Kulu from a common herb, which proves efficacious in "stealing away men's brains."

At night each party bivouacs out, there being much feasting and more noise round a fire; the din gradually becomes less and the debauchery greater, being only comparable to a small "Barthelemy Fair." It is a great pity this "religious meeting" could not be transferred for three days to Exeter Hall.

The Devil's avocations are not, however, limited to these two great "Malees." He must keep the

THE DEVIL GOD

Kell Broˢ Lith

RIESON TEA GARDEN.

"wallet" full at any cost. If it rains too much, or does not rain at all, he can find an excuse, and out the whole procession comes, climbing the mountain side, and turning out the farmer's wife something in this way: "No rain! who wonders at it? You had large crops last time, and never send Davi a bit of corn. Your sheep dropped plenty, but you never send the Devil one lamb. Now I want one rupee eight annas. Ah! it's of no use your saying you have only a rupee in the world; I'll soon turn up the pot underground with the money in it. I've spoken to the Devil, and he says it is such as you that keep the rain away. Speak again? Well, I will; but you must give me one of those new shawls for the cold weather, and ten seers of fine flour, and then I'll speak to the Devil for you about the weather." This is really the kind of thing that goes on, the villagers having the greatest terror of Davi and the priests, and yet it is no more than Captain Marryat describes, and I have heard preached by the illiterate negroes in the West Indies. "Aye, Mr. Butcher, you kill sheep twice a week, and neber send me one bit of 'libber.' Wha you tink you go to?"

That thing you see on wheels on the Maidan in front of the rest-house, is the car which carries the Kulu Devil or Juggernaut about on these occasions; but his holiness is not like the others, it is a gold bcx, or a gold image in a box. I have only seen the latter, and when this was brought up the hill from the temple in the city, and deposited in this carriage, which is all covered with crimson and gold, the late Rae made his obeisance to it, and presented some gold mohurs. It was then surrounded by the attendants and priests, and dragged by a number of Kulu people all over the Maidan, visiting the wealthy who were encamped in handsome tents, and no doubt had to "shell out" the pecuniary gratification for the ever-hungry Davi, who with all his influence, as they believe, with the clerk of the weather, cannot always prevent a shower of rain putting the whole community, which may at times be estimated at 6000 people, into one general *sauve qui peut* to get under shelter.

The appearance of the several processions leaving on the last day is very picturesque, as they wind up the mountain sides in all directions, drums beating, flags flying, and heads aching if not hearts.

The following account is from Fergusson's 'Picturesque Architecture of Hindostan,' page 25:—

"The images of the gods (Jugganath at Puri) are placed on a throne in the dark chamber under the great tower, where, of course, they are not visible to Europeans; but they are brought out once a year, when all the world may feast their eyes on their hideousness, and it would perhaps be difficult to imagine a scene in which the ludicrous and absurd so completely overpowers the sublimity that must always accompany an earnest act of adoration on the part of a hundred thousand human beings, who are usually congregated there on these occasions. The image of Jugganath is a single block of wood, 6 feet in length and about the same in girth, formed into a bust. As long as his progress is down the steps of the temple all goes on smoothly, but as the block is of some weight it is no such easy matter to get him through the deep mud of the level

street. To effect this the lower part of the image is always somewhat rounded, and the attendants swing him backwards and forwards till the oscillatory motion is deemed sufficient, when those in front, who have hold on a rope which is tied round his waist, give a pull, those behind a push, and his godship is thus hitched on a few yards, when there is a pause to allow the chowrie-bearers to flap away the flies and the fan-bearers to cool the god after the exertion.

"Then another pull and a swing, a shove and a shout; and this is repeated again and again, till he is dragged up the inclined plane into his car. His chest, containing all his requisites for his journey, is then brought forth (in size and appearance very like a midshipman's sea-chest of the present day). In this are not only his clothes and food, but his *hands* and *feet*, which *he* uses as we mortals do our boots and gloves,—to be put on only when wanted; and after being washed and dressed, he should of course proceed on his journey. The fates, however, were not propitious to the poor god, for the next morning his car had only advanced a few yards, and stuck fast in the mud on the spot where I sketched it on the following day. That night it ran up against a house, and as there are no means of turning the car, they were obliged to *pull the house down* and pass over the ruins; and as besides this the roads were heavy, the god was three days in reaching his country-house, the Goundicha Nour, at the distance of half a mile from the temple."

Kulu men are allowed more wives than one, and as the females do most of the field labour except ploughing, the more wives a man can provide for, the better he gets off. At the same time some women marry several husbands. When at Manali I was told of one who married three brothers, but the youngest soon destroyed himself from jealousy. Certain it is that the ladies are more notorious for their fine figures and faces than for their virtue; and more than one "officer on leave" has got a wigging for casting "sweet glances" at them, by the late censor of morals, the former Assistant-Commissioner of Kulu, which, however, was not entirely approved by Lord Mayo.

Kell, Bro^{s} Lith.

THE SILVER TIARA—A NATIVE LADY.

The head-dress of the women is very picturesque, and the English fashion may be supposed to have been copied from the manner in which they wear the little round scarlet cap on the very front of their forehead over their eyes, a style universally adopted in England lately.

On the occasion of one Mela I was permitted to take sketches of some of those whose dress I considered the most characteristic or picturesque.

The men, as well as women, are often seen spinning even as they travel along the road, and their clothes are nicely made up by the women; they wear a crimson or black woollen skull-cap with a roll round the head, and usually some straw ornament or flower on the left side. Their thick woollen clothes are usually fastened by large silver pins, and nearly everyone wears a jewel of silver with a figure of a devil enamelled in blue on it, a style of work they are very clever in. Their faith seems to be, keep on good terms with the devil, God will never do you any harm.

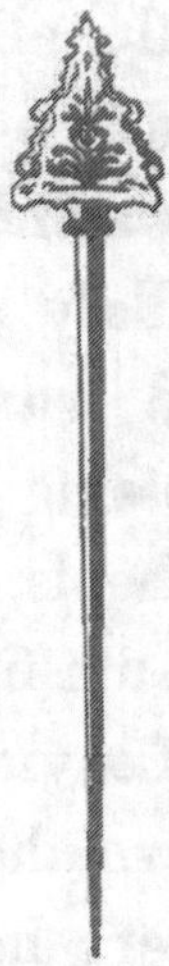

They make snow-shoes of straw in a very ingenious way, and these are even preferred by Europeans when sporting on the snowy hills; but strong stockings or socks must be worn with them.

A good trade is done here at times, especially in the autumn, when the Yarkandee merchants arrive with their goods to exchange for European. There is a great trade also in borax, some of which is purified in the lower bazaar before being sent to the plains; carpets, churus, and even gold is brought from the plains beyond Lahoul, where there are as many as 1500 persons employed at the diggings for six months in the year.

The appearance of the Yarkandees and Lahoul people is not prepossessing, the latter especially are most disgusting,—being filthy, dirty, and forward to impudence, as well as drunken; they hang about Kulu all the winter to the annoyance of everyone and the danger of movable commodities. I found it was not safe to pass through them without a fair shillaly at hand, or even something more effective, and was once nearly pulled from my pony while crossing the Sultanpur Maidan by a drunken lot of Lahouls, who escaped for want of something more than a fist to mark them with.

Leaving the rest-house at Sultanpur we proceed down the road into the lower bazaar and bed of the river: here are some very fine citron trees; and the view of the bridges, as we near the river, is very pretty.

The ascent to the town is not quite so bad as the descent on the other side; the Post Office is in a *hole* in the entrance gate, and the postmaster is obliged, by *virtue of his office* (?), to live in the room above, up a ladder.

THE LAHOUL BAZAAR BELOW SULTANPUR ON THE BEAS.

No stamps are sold at the Post Office, you must go to the Tehseel, where, like myself on more occasions than one, you may have to wait for days before anyone attends to sell them, or even to answer the door. I have known a tourist detained five days here before he could change a money-order; and I know for a fact that the poor Dak runners who have to pass over from Kulu to Palumpore every day, all weathers, had not received a pice of pay for six months when I left!

The Tehseel of Kulu comprises Kulu Proper and Vazeeri Rupi; contains 46,000 inhabitants, 3000 of which are in Vazeeri Rupi, and 1110 in the town of Sultanpur.

The inhabitants are quiet and peaceable, if not industrious; like many other natives, however, the presence of the Commissioner incites them to litigation, which, but for the opportunity, they would not indulge in. The Kutcherry to them is like the law court or the whisky shop to an Irishman: he cannot pass the one without having a "drop of potheen," and he is never happy unless he has some lawsuit on the tapis, especially about an inch of "land," for which it is notorious either of them would "sell his soul."

There is a fair school whose pupils learn cricket among other things; and in '69 there was an educational officer on Rs. 800 per mensem resident in the valley to look after the pupils.

A serai has lately been erected by Government

with the aid of *forced* labour! for the Yarkand people visiting Kulu; but it is very unhealthy, being down in a complete swamp, whose deadly malaria carries off the stray population every autumn after the rains; this might be drained at a trifling cost if the convicts were not so hard-worked at that garlic and green peas in the Tehseel garden.

Sultanpur is 4092 feet above sea level, Bijli 8070, and those high peaks over the river to the right, "Krinchall" or Milander Peak, 11,443; and the farther one, "Rumetu," 12,084.

The large tree on the summit of the ridge opposite Sultanpur can be seen from Karowne ten miles up the Sivbarri River or Bubu Khud, and on the opposite side from the Parbutti mountains and valley.

The right bank or west side of the river Beas is the most agreeable to travel the next stage, the road being wide and good, and for the most part offering a pleasant view, especially of the richly-wooded islands in the river and the opposite bank.

As we ascend the valley, the idea of its once having been a great glacier or lake becomes more apparent and decided.

Just as we are about to rise a second time from the edge of the river, and about six miles from Sultanpur, we see, peeping over the top of the hill on the left, the pretty cottage of Bundrole, built at great cost by a retired officer for his residence; the ascent is somewhat steep, but those who have his acquaintance are amply compensated for the climb by the happiness of his agreeable society.

There was above his house, some height up, a landslip, of which the native tradition is as follows :—

One evening an old woman came to the village that was there two or three years ago only, and demanded shelter for the night; this was, however, refused her, and she cursed the village, and went to the hut of a Dagi, or low-caste man, in another village a little lower down the hill, who extended to her the hospitality she had in vain sought at the first village. On her asking for some milk the Dagi lamented that he had none to give her. The old woman then desired him to go and look in the stable; he did so, and there found a beautiful white cow that he had never seen before, and whose milk not only supplied the old woman, but also himself and his family, a very unusual thing in this land of small and but little milk-giving cattle.

In the morning the old woman and cow had both disappeared, and the village above had been destroyed by a landslip, of which the site is still visible. The natives say this woman was the "Spirit of the Mountain."

Three miles farther up the river, the next house is seen above a small and young tea plantation; this is Rieson, the property of the same tea proprietors whose success here is not better than at other places. The house is rather in a hole, and too much surrounded by paddy fields, or it would be a desirable spot.

A little farther on, and close on the road, is "Dobie House," and the camping ground opposite. This house is usually let to some visitor every year.

Opposite is the bridge over the river, leading to Nugger, but there is no rest-house or accommodation other than space to pitch your tent there, and hardly that; but for tourists not returning down the valley it is better to take this road to Nugger, and to camp at Jugget Sookht, or even cross to Manali, but it is a long march,—but a much better road than our present one along the river, where the view is confined.

A few miles from Dobie are the hot springs, where is also a camping ground. These springs and baths are in great repute and use with the natives, but have a very foul smell, the water never being emptied entirely out, however many natives may use it in a day. The spring evidently emanates from the decomposition of sulphuret pyrites in the adjoining metamorphic rock. There are others at Bahist farther on, which we shall refer to.

The road now continues along the river banks, shaded by numberless trees, but is neither too wide nor too smooth. After passing a temporary bridge across, the river from Jugget Sookht runs into the Beas with great force, and on to a sloping bed; and the effect of the thickly-wooded bank and the foaming

REST HOUSE AT MANALI, KULU

water rushing down the rocky bed is something really charming. It is a great pity Bourne and Shephard, when they were in this valley taking views, had no one to point out to them this and similar beauties of Nature to copy, whereas some of those they did photograph are places of little or no beauty or interest.

We still continue along this shady road by the river side, till a sudden rise brings you into the Deodar forest of Manali, which is gradually yielding to the axe of the Forest Department, as it did years ago to that of the Sikhs.

Here is a modest little rest-house, which, however, is not available if the Assistant-Commissioner is residing in the valley, for, though he has Nugger Castle, all the rest-houses are claimed by him also for offices.

In the forest on the adjacent hill-side, hid in a mass of huge Deodar pines, is the Temple of Dungree, of which I have made a sketch on the occasion of a large festival and sacrifice in 1869, when a buffalo and 150 sheep and goats were sacrificed in front to the Davi or Juggernath, or Devil God.

This building is almost entirely of Deodar timber, and is erected over a huge naturally projecting rock, which is often the case; but there is nothing inside worth seeing.

The temple is said to be over 600 years old. The front is elaborately carved, but some of the subjects are so grossly indecent they could not be copied. This filthy indecency and many others are particularly protected by a special clause in the Penal Code that permits the public exhibition of statues, carving, or pictures, of the most libidinous kind, provided they are connected with some religious temple or worship.

The sacrifice in this instance took place under the patronage of a European, but not an Englishman.

The people having assembled from all parts of the valley and adjacent villages, dressed in their handsomest dresses and jewels, some of which are of no mean value, the headmen and priests assembled in front of the temple amid the shouts of the people, the bellowing of trumpets and horns, the shrill screech of the pipe, and the beating of drums and cymbals.

Having cleared half a circle round the door, on the left of which sat our German patron, the priests sat down on the stone-paved ground, and began chanting and jabbering some invocation to the Devil God that I could not understand. To increase their excitement, a dish—always provided and carried before the god—was brought, and fire put in it; on the fire a quantity of some wild herb was thrown, which produced volumes of smoke, over which the performers held their heads till the blood came into their eyes and an intoxicated excitement overcame them. Suddenly they all let their long hair fall loose and shook it over their faces, and swung their heads round and

SACRIFICE AT DUNGREE TEMPLE.

round, giving them a most demoniacal expression. Presently the buffalo was brought up, and I left the place. As I descended the hill I heard the repeated *thuds* of the heavy cutlass and other weapons on the devoted buffalo, who was eventually "hacked to pieces"; the shrieks of the females, compelled to look on, the noise of drums, and shouting were deafening, and I am told by a Eurasian, who was there, that he nearly fainted from the sickness at the sight before he could manage to extricate himself from the crowd, the whole place flowing with blood.

At the Vindhyachal Fair, Mirzapore, "hundreds of goats and bullocks were sacrificed" (see *Pioneer*, 8th March, 1871). In what way has a Christian Government done its duty, to leave these people in a state of semi-barbarism thus?

Yet I was threatened with the vengeance of Government if I dare to kill a beef at Christmas!

After the sacrifice, the whole people removed farther up the hill, where, still under the delightful shade of the forest, they indulged in racing, wrestling, scrambling, and jumping.

The gay attire of the females, who sat on a raised dais or amphitheatre of stone—a sort of private or "dress circle"—was nicely contrasted against the dark foliage of the trees behind, and the gay drapery and silver ornaments of the visiting Davis added to the brilliancy of the scene. At short distances in the more retired parts of the forest were placed the

"Toddy" shops, for the sale of bang or other intoxicating liquors, and worse purposes.

I was much struck with the head-dresses in particular of some of the females and the good looks of the greater part, had they not all suffered from so much exposure in the air. One old lady I sat behind was wrinkled like a tortoise, and seemed about eighty years of age, not having apparently a tooth in her head. On her loosening the silver pin of her shawl to accept some sweets offered her, you may imagine my surprise at seeing she was suckling a young baby, and at her side her young married daughter, about fourteen, was doing the same natural office for her child.

The boys enjoyed the sport, but the girls could not be induced to join in any, further than holding up their hands to catch any of the copper coins thrown for a scramble, and altogether generally the females showed great modesty and sobriety during the day: but some were much puzzled to get their tipsy husbands safe home. The nights, I am told, were a scene of debauchery with those who stayed to "keep it up." All this took place within a short distance of the Assistant-Commissioner's camp.

The carving round the balcony of the adjoining "Ranee's old palace" is amusing; particularly one panel representing the Luchme Narayon.

Luchme Narayon, an avatar or incarnation of Vishnu, in which he descended to punish one of

GODDESS BOWANNE ATPOOGEE.

BAS-RELIEF IN MICACEOUS SLATE IN RECESS BAJAURA TEMPLE, KULU.

Page 16.

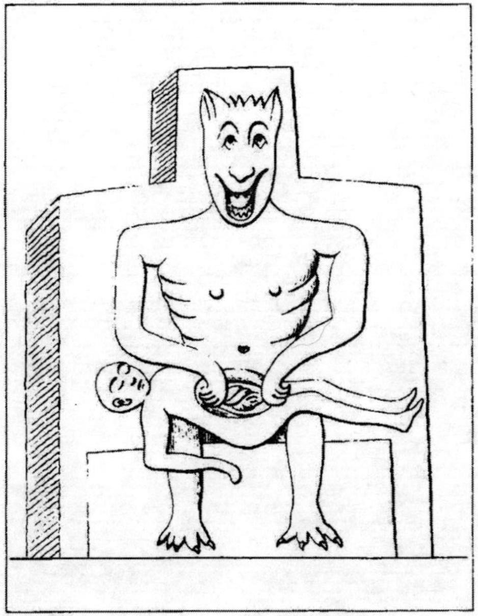

LUCHME NARAYON.

CARVED IN WOOD. DUNJREE.

Page [illegible]

J. Calvert

the kings of Rajasthan. The king defied Vishnu's power, and was about to put his own son to death for remonstrating, when Vishnu appeared as Luchme Narayon in the form of a tiger out of one of the pillars of the palace and chawed up the impious king.

The village of Manali is higher up north at the mouth of the khud where are the ruins of the old fort, destroyed probably during the first invasion of Kulu some two hundred and seventy years ago, at least so the late Rae Jyan Singh told me. This, and the fort at Bajaura, and the old Tehseel and garden at Sultanpur, and some three thousand acres of the best land in Kulu, are the property of General Sir Arthur Cunnynghame, and his partners in the "Kulu Tea Estate."

The view of the snow-covered mountains north of this shows the regular stratification of their formation, and contrasts well with the rich dark tints of the splendid Deodar forests beneath, the prime of which are being annually cut down and launched into the river to float down to the plains for the constant demand for railway sleepers.

This is the most northerly slide for timber in Kulu, as it will not pass the river higher up.

Continuing on this pleasant ride still in the forest we cross the bridge over Manali Khud, and in a short time will be observed and for some time—high up on the perpendicular mountains to the right—several beautiful waterfalls that ever and anon disappear in a crevice to start forth lower down with increased volume and more foaming spray.

The next stage is to Rolla, but there is a rest-house at Pulchan, which is not, however, a desirable resting place—the flies being as bad as a pestilence from the number of Lahoul sheep and goats that encamp here on their way up and down the valley.

Here and at Manali ice can be had with ease, and with the wild strawberries make delicious ices.

The immense number of granite and gneiss boulders here excite attention, and the fine specimens of black tourmalins in some of them; they are much water-worn, and some of immense dimensions. There is a magnificent forest up a khud which joins the Sahari Khud at Pulchan, where one would suspect these stones to have come from, yet, strange to say, the hills above are all of a different "formation."

At Pulchan I had the pleasure of meeting the son of Longfellow the poet, whose shattered frame told of that bitter struggle in the Southern States. He was on his way to Cashmere, with many others. About 150 visitors pass through Kulu every year.

Over this river is Solang, the most northerly village in Kulu. In the forest near here was a Deodar tree 150 feet long and 18 feet girth.

Here also are much iron pyrites, reported to Government as gold, and the ruin of many a one who has resigned all his certain prospects in life for a heap of glittering rubbish and want!!

Kell, Bro^s lith.

KULU WOMEN AT MANALI FAIR_ A LIKENESS.

The village over the river opposite the rest-house is Pulchan, but the other just over the bridge is "Rewa."

Here I used to indulge daily in strawberry ices. The fruit grows wild as well as in gardens, and the snow ice can be had quite close up the shady khud.

A little beyond this village, where the road is cut in the solid rock, is an excavation used as the last habitation in Kulu, on the highway, and one that the authorities should suppress, being the lowest kind of grog shop where the passing Lahoulies are enticed to drink to excess, and I have seen them when leaving within an inch of being precipitated down the perpendicular precipice below, there being no wall or fence to save them, and I was told more than one had met the fate of being dashed to pieces in the torrent below.

Crossing the bridge at Pulchan we commence a short, but the best stage for scenery in Kulu, between this and Rolla; the rock over the bridge is remarkable for the zigzag appearance of its stratification, which is the same all over it from top to bottom. After reaching the top or level of this road, there is at a small distance a very interesting gorge or mere crevice in the rock below, in which all the water of the river passes; and farther on the waterfalls and scenery are admired by all.

Near here, of course, are the sources of the Beas River, some of which fall with picturesque effect from a considerable height.

Rotang Mountain is 15,206 feet above sea level.

The ascent of Rotang Pass, 13,330, is tedious but not difficult, but many tourists go no farther, though many others continue on that way to Cashmere. It was crossing here, and re-crossing the same day, that affected Lord Elgin to his death.

His Lordship had to pass over the river to Kokser in a basket suspended on a rope of twigs; since then a timber bridge has been built, which is certainly far better, bad as it is.

There is a road from the Rotang Pass to Spiti and Shigri on the east, along the Chundra Valley, but as it is out of repair we will propose returning, unless that desolate country Lahoul, which you see before you, tempts you to pass over.

We will therefore retrace our steps to Pulchan for the night and enjoy some ice-creams, and contemplate how these miles of large boulders were deposited here, and from where they came.

That large glacier over the river in front of the Pass is the "Sona-pani."

I previously made an inquiring allusion to the suggestion of this valley having at one time been a large glacier like those on the surrounding mountains, and as the climate has altered, which has evidently been the case, the ice has melted into a lake of water. Travellers now alive remember lakes in the mountains here now dried up. In this state it must have received that deep deposit of boulders which can be seen more than one hundred feet deep from Bajara upwards as far as Manali, but how or where these boulders came from — all of hard rocks worn round as we are apt to say by attrition—is a question that has puzzled many, who content themselves with the remark, "they were deposited during *the glacial period*"—a period supposed by some to have marked the close of the last "tertiary age" previous to the creation of Historic Man. The forces that must have been employed for ages to grind these masses of the hardest rocks into their rounded shapes were something far more powerful and of longer endurance than the mere journey from the top of a modern glacier. For instance, see the rocks up the Shigri Glacier, some lying on the surface of the ice not far from the top, which is not far from 20,000 feet high, are already round, but the masses that are now day by day descending in that enormous stream of ice, which is over 200 feet thick and a mile or more across,—these are not round, but the greatest portion of them as square or sharp as when they separated from their parent mountain. That the stream of ice continues in motion I *proved by careful observation*, but there seemed no motion in any portion of such glacier—on which I spent many hours on several occasions—to account for the great attrition necessary to produce such rounding results. Even in the case of the rocks decomposing, they usually do so according to their sedimentary deposit or formation; even granite will decompose more in one direction than another, especially as the climate or conditions affect the potass in the component parts, the feldspar, and the mica. Besides, huge rounded boulders of gneiss are met with at the top of Hamta Pass above the clayslate and sandstone, with which they have no affinity or connection, and may be found on the summits of still higher mountains close by. That they have been ejected from volcanoes is a favourite theory, but in theory we do not find the ejections from volcanoes to be rounded rocks, but rather the reverse, sharp-pointed fragments of all shapes and sizes, except lavas, &c.; but gneiss boulders could not have been ejected in a lava or molten state, and still retain the original stratification of its ingredients. Besides, there are immense masses of metamorphic rocks scattered about, which are still harder of texture, and though they seem to have been affected by the like corrosion to a certain degree, are seldom seen so round.

To those who have seen the moon through the most powerful telescopes in the world, it is apparent that the surface of that luminary is covered with them of all sizes, as was, in all probability, this world, when in a *similar* condition at the epoch of the second day's creation.

There can be little doubt, in my opinion, that the water or ice, or both, were confined, in distant ages, close to Largi at the bottom of the valley, if not as

DOWN KULU VALLEY FROM MANALI FOREST.

well as Jhirri, from whence the waters may have overrun into the lower lake, the bottom of which appears to be a conglomerate of various limestones similar to that which forms the upper part of the rocks adjacent. On bursting of these "bunds" the floods have actually cut a river through this conglomerate more than a hundred and fifty feet deep below Badool in Bilan Koti, near the new bridge or ferry, and in the upper part through the boulders and loose conglomerate seen on either side all up the valley.

That the climate has altered in comparatively modern times is plain, as snow is never known to lie now in nullahs which bear the marks of being worn by destructive glaciers and torrents that carried enormous blocks of stone before them with the greatest ease.

We now propose to retrace our steps to Manali at least, but if we can, to cross over to Bahist to the hot springs and baths. If not, we must cross at Manali and return to them. There is space at Bahist to camp out, and ladies sometimes indulge in a few days' bathing here, but as they are, to a certain degree, sulphur springs, no one should use them without medical advice. The heat of the water is 120°, but is cooler in the centre of the bath, which is of stone, and when I visited them they were clean, and could be enclosed private.

The road was but in bad condition at that time, but the distance is small.

There are plenty of bears about Manali in the day time; they come for the fruit, especially those blue plums; there are also leopards at night. In the hills are chikor and the famous Minal pheasant, as well as others. Fine fish are also netted here.

To gentlemen who have time, a trip to the Hamta Pass will amply repay, especially in July and August, when they can witness a sight of flowers unequalled anywhere, though very fine on the Rotang Pass.

From Manali, crossing the Beas by the bridge below, the village of Prini is about two miles; the ascent is by a zigzag road through the forest on the spur of a hill between two khuds, one of which to the left is the Raini Khud, the other on the right is of minor importance, called the Phari Khud.

There is a temple under some large banyan trees half-way up, which I regret I did not examine, but the remainder of the road leads you first into one khud and then into the other, till the village at the top is reached, and this is called Hamta; this is near the top or rather the level, and is the last habitable place in this direction on account of the winter snow. Just above, the traveller is delighted to find a delicious spring of water, and I could suggest any liberal person who goes that way, may immortalize himself by erecting a roof over the same and be blessed by every passer-by.

The ascent now ceases; there is no more climbing, and you may progress easily on horse or foot, for the

Kell, Bro[s] lith.

MANALI PEASANTS

road is good to Cheeken ten miles or less; but you must turn round and look, before the valley of Kulu is hid from your view. Notice how each delta, or junction of the tributary streams on either side of the Beas, is thick with trees, the seeds brought down from the khuds and here propagated; the whole valley to Sultanpur is here exhibited in one fair view that is delightful to behold.

On the left the snow-topped mountains exhibit a somewhat regular slope, showing the dip of the formation, which is mostly sandstone, the villages occasionally dotting their sides, peeping out of the rich forests that cover the valley sides; while the varied colours of the produce of the fields contrast with harmony. The red rice, the white opium, the yellow corn, and the red poppy, with here and there the verdant grass, or new-ploughed earth, show the industry of the inhabitant, and the richness of the soil.

One cannot, however, but miss the hedge that should define each field; yet you do not see cattle straying, probably more from fear of their hides, than honesty of desire, for they are mostly like skeletons, so poorly are cattle cared for by the natives in India.

But to return to our journey from Prini to the Raini Khud.

Now we enter forests of immense pine-trees, and see the gorgeous blaze of numberless flowers that cover the ground for miles, as if we were entering some fairy gardens.

What a site for a residence and a park, but six months' snow render it uninhabitable.

Here I feel my ignorance, but the botanist would revel amid the numberless indigenous flowers of every hue, the sunflower, the balsam, alike six feet high or more, and a thousand others, each vieing with the other to be the tallest and the loveliest.

Sunflowers grow to an enormous size in Kulu, and are said to purify the air and make it healthy. It is fine feeding for poultry when in seed, and yields 15 per cent. of oil and 15 cwt. of seed per acre. Yet it is not cultivated.

The river is out of sight, if not hearing, low down in the khud, on the north side of which the proud rock stands erect for miles, as if guardian of the privacy of this lovely valley.

Once or twice small streams are crossed by bridges.

At the upper part of the valley are the birch-trees, from the bark of which is separated the papyrus used so much about this part for paper and packing, and by the ancients and some isolated people for books and writing; this is never found lower than 5000 feet above the sea. Most of the trees here are bent low down by the weight of the snow on them in the winter.

Now a long narrow bridge or plank crosses the Raini stream, and we come upon that pretty waterfall at Cheeken, and the large loose rocks that form the only shelter to the poor passing shepherds, who bring their flocks this way to pasture during the hot weather between this and the mountains of Spiti.

And here the fuel is cut to smelt the ores from the Shigri Mines in Chundra Valley.

You can either camp here or three miles farther on, but this is decidedly the best place if the ground is cleared.

Now we have to pass that jumble of rocks called by me "the Gorge," where the rush of water between and over the enormous blocks of detached stone would make a splendid photograph or painting. On account of the shade covering the stream here the ice is never entirely melted, but the water finds its way through underneath.

The footpath is but indifferent here for horses, which should in fact be left here, or sent to Prini, for several reasons.

Here you must collect fuel for the rest of your trip and provisions for all who accompany you, as nothing but milk and occasionally a goat or sheep can be obtained till you get to Spiti, and for that you must give notice some time before at Jugget Sookht or to the Assistant-Commissioner at Nugger Castle.

The distant view of "snowy peak pillar" and the peaks above the Hamta Pass are seen from here to great advantage.

When camping out here, my attention was called

to some object moving the foliage beneath a large boulder close to my tent. At first I expected to find a snake, but, after driving in every direction, a small pair of conies came out; they were about five or six inches long, but unlike any I have seen before. On my return I found them dead, apparently from the rain, for it was not cold.

The upper Raini Valley contains much of interest, and in several places the remains of the winter glaciers may be seen occasionally, with large rocks resting on the top of the unmelted mass of ice and gravel brought down from above, and still twenty or thirty feet thick; at times may be seen one large boulder mounted on a pillar of ice, which is gradually getting smaller and smaller as the mid-day sun shines on it, while on its summit a mass of smaller stones and gravel show, when imbedded in the glacier now melted, the water carried a debris over its top.

Here may be found some valuable gems, if you know where to seek them, and are provided with proper tools—and *patience*—to cut them out of their stone matrix.

I have found sapphires there worth Rs. 2500 each, besides other gems.

It is best to ascend the Hamta Pass, 14,500, as early as you can, as the approaches are less wet, and the ice, if any, on the upper part less soft. This Pass is slightly below the perpetual snow line. The shingle and small streams of water are not favourable

Kell, Bros. Lith. London.

DEOBITA 20,000 FT. — NORTH SIDE HAMTA PASS. 14,700 FT.

to boots of any but the thickest kind, but it requires no very great exertion to reach the summit. It is advisable to have a guide with you and at times holding on, for I have seen one or two unexpected descents to the bottom in a rapid slide on the back after having spent half an hour in getting up. The sheep and goat track is the safest, and if you should meet a flock, always let them pass first, for they run with such determined force, especially if loaded, that you are easily carried off your legs if you come in contact with them.

When near the summit of this Pass, the path lies over the solid ice and snow, and it requires great care to prevent slipping, as the ascent is a steep slope. On my return this way, one of my natives slipped and slid down a great distance, and narrowly escaped going down a narrow crevice, which he would have found difficult to get out of.

Here I would advise the tourist about to ascend a height not to take spirits, a few cocoa nibs are the finest things for the breath, and are habitually used by the South Americans and Mexicans when climbing any considerable steep. On the summit, previous to descending, a peg may not do harm.

The Coca.—This is a very remarkable plant in its effects upon the human constitution. The natives in several parts of Peru chew its leaves as Europeans do tobacco, particularly in the mining districts, when at work in the mines or travelling; and such is the sustenance derived from them, that they frequently take no food for four or five days.

I have often been assured by them that while they have a good supply of coca, they feel neither hunger, thirst, nor fatigue; and, without impairing their health, they can remain eight or ten days and nights without sleep.

The leaves are almost insipid; but when a small quantity of lime is mixed with them, they have an agreeable sweet taste. The natives generally carry with them a leather pouch of coca and a small calabash holding lime, or the ashes of the molle, to mix with them.

The view from the top of the "Hamta Pass" down the Hamta Valley, and of the "Kazaling" Glacier and snowy peaks in Lahoul, is surpassing grand, and repays one the little exertion, for it is of easy ascent this way compared with the other side, which is a stiff pull from the Chundra River, now far below what can be seen in the distance. Here you have "all the world before you" and a great deal below you. Bourne and Shephard have a splendid photograph of this wild scene, No. 1445.

To the left, but at present out of sight, are two very steep glaciers of ice, at least I never heard of them being entirely melted, down which occasionally large rocks slide or roll with wonderful celerity, and it is well to keep one's eye looking up as you pass them, and dig your boots and alpenstock well in at every step.

The second time I passed, I preferred to do so by going down to the bed of the river: and this is the path that yaks and ponies take, especially when ascending.

The road then comes very easy for some distance, and there are places where you can camp out or get temporary shelter under the rocks, as the "Guddees" do while pasturing their sheep.

At last you begin to descend rapidly, and have to cross a frail bridge over a deep torrent to the right bank of the stream, and a continued descent brings you in half an hour to Chutrâ, another camping place among the rocks; there is, however, room for a tent among the beds of flowers that blaze a violet blue. I found no other colour here.

The Chundra River is now at your feet, and Lahoul as near as you desire *that* part to be.

This is the usual camping place; and now we are "beyond the rainy season," they say it never rains here, if not I will be bound it *snows* occasionally.

From here to Shigri is a day's good march, but there are resting grounds about four miles, and at Futta Rine* on this side of the Burra Shigri River, another over the Shigri River, and a fourth three miles farther at the Shigri Mines on this side the great Shigri Glacier. It is well to note these places, which are known to the men and guides.

Soon after leaving Chutrâ you descend to the

* Or "Footch Rhoon," the cleft rock.

banks of the river, but ascend again to cross the stream that comes from the melting of the "glacier" above, and the higher you ascend to cross, the easier you get over, and the nearer view you get of the interesting mass of ice above.

It must be remarked that the streams from this glacier fall down so steep an incline that they bring with them heaps of stones; these form the bed which constantly increases in height, that the stream eventually is carried in a trough of stones much higher than the adjacent ground, and is comparatively confined in a narrow channel, but lower down this is burst open and scattered, and the stream divides into many branches of far greater width than depth, and when reaching the sand at the bottom it is dangerous, being "quick." Your foot once set on that sinks with a surer fatality than in water, and closes over you without hope in a few seconds.

You then proceed along the bed of the river for some distance, gradually turning to the right up the bed of another torrent from the "Sackchum Glacier," which fortunately is easily passed by a natural bridge of the rocks, amongst which the water rushes with great fury from a large glacier above; on ascending the opposite bank you may contemplate the gigantic blocks of stone that lie tumbled about as if they had been mere logs of wood. One of these both by shape and size appears like a good-sized two-roomed cottage with a gable at each end.

On the summits of the largest of these you will usually see small stones or flags of rag placed by the first natives who have passed in the season, though I can imagine that some of these relics endure the effects of a winter's snow without being removed.

Here is a lovely little Maidan to camp on, nice water, and pretty flowers worth taking back.

I never saw much shooting in this valley, indeed a place so devoid of vegetation and so truly lonely one seldom sees in any country, as these few miles, but there is something awfully grand as you look back on the Hamta Pass from here.

From here we again descend to the river bed, but if a road could—and I am convinced it is possible—be made a moderate way up the side of the hill, the very worst part of the journey would be escaped, for the clambering over the loose boulders and rocks may be, and evidently is, easy enough for goats, sheep, and yaks, but for bipeds it keeps one's feet and legs in considerable jeopardy, to say nothing of one's head,—and tail. I shall never forget my pony clattering over and in between them so much to the distress of his shins, that he asked not to be brought again.

At last you reach Futta Rine,* which is distinguished by only one or two very large stones over twenty feet high, which form a natural kitchen, and are useful as a shelter. If you camp here you can get to the mines in about three hours easily.

* Mr. A. G. Young calls it Footeh Rhoon, or the "cleft rock."

But if you do not mean to stay at the mines, but cross the great glacier, try and get on—or anyhow let the crossing the glacier be the first task of a day, as it is an awful "grind."

On the left of Futta Rine the mountains in Lahoul have a most grotesque appearance. On the right or facing is the Burra Shigri River and khud. The usual bridge, two frail planks, but by sanding the soles of the feet you get a good and safe footing across. And here we are in "Shigri" camping ground, but it's no use staying—move on, and in two hours we are at another little grass plot surrounded with huge boulders, and a nice flat table stone in the centre. Here we make a grand stand and take a hearty breakfast, but look all round, and at the map. On calling for my pony here one day I was greatly astonished at seeing the syce and him emerge from a deep hole among the closely adjacent rocks, where I found he had roomy quarters, and almost enough for two.

It had been known for many years, and especially by the natives that travelled this way, that large lumps of antimony were found on and near the road farther on and about here, but the actual lode from whence these were carried periodically by the winter's ice and snow had never been ascertained.

To discover this was the object of my journey, and accompanied only by a few natives to carry my camp, I started on what my friends called a "wild-goose chase." With pick and gad and a few drills I searched the steep mountain side for some time in vain, but experience in such work, and the determination to take root on the spot rather than not succeed, prevented even a thought of failure, and ensured success.

Having enlisted a herd of Lahoul people, we ascended the hill the first day without more success than collecting a large quantity of loose pieces of ore, some of which were too large for our combined forces to move till broken up by sledge hammers. Next day, higher up, I found indications, which eventually led me to the exposed face of a lode of solid ore from ten to twenty feet wide. This I soon opened, and every "kilter" was rapidly filled, and as much again over and over thrown down hill to the road, where it was collected, the refuse being abandoned, and only the pure ores taken away,* namely, the stibnite or sulphuret of antimony and the red and yellow ores. This, when reduced to *Regulus*, can be shipped home for 32*l*. per ton, including every cost, and sells there for 76*l*. per ton: after eighteen months' delay the Government granted a lease on very liberal terms, and it is hoped, by means of capitalists at home, to commence working these mines very shortly. The Government generously forgave the usual stamp on this lease, it being the first mineral (metallic) lease ever granted in India.

* There is another lode I am sure, but more to the east and high up.

Since this was in type, Mr. A. G. Young has verified the above,* and found a lode of black antimony, or stibnite, to the east higher up, a little to the left, and assures me there are marks of where the lode was blasted. This was done by order of Major Hay about eighteen years ago, and accounts for the quantity of loose ore found on the hill-side. Mr. Young describes the new lode which I opened as forty feet wide, the lode of solid metallic ore in the centre being at least twenty feet wide. This lode can be easily quarried without any blasting, being in laminated beds easily separated by bars and wedges. The scoriæ, or froth, at the top of the lode is remarkable, consisting of the oxide (cervantite), a yellow mineral, and the bright red (kermesite), with some little iron. It has all the appearance of being the result of igneous action.

This lode is peculiar, as exhibiting little or no gneiss rock blended with the ore, whereas the other lode of black radiating stibnite abounds in places with sulphuret of iron and crystals of zinc-blende, the whole penetrating the rock in places to a great depth, showing they must all have been, at a time, in a molten state.

To any adventurous shikaree, who desires to immortalize himself, there is a capital opportunity afforded by finding a path from Burra Shigri or Futta Rine to the Malauna Khud and on to the "Holy City of Manikarn." This could only be

* September, 1872.

Kell Bros Lith. London.

VIEW OF LAHOUL FROM KANSAM PASS — 14,931 FT

done, I expect, about August and September, or even October. It does not look inviting, but it is said that some Guddees have *done* the road once, and if the pasturage would tempt *them*, surely the ibex and other game should tempt the English sportsman.

There is not much to be said respecting the road farther on to Chota Shigri, Kansam Pass, and Spiti. After crossing the glacier which occupies two or three hours' jumping and climbing, the road is, with one or two exceptions, easier than the one we have come; and the top of Kansam Pass is a large level covered with thousands of mementos raised by travellers that have passed, some of which must have cost much time and labour to have built up. The natives consider this practice as in some way meritorious.

The road through Spiti and round back to Simla is interesting, to the geologist in particular, some of the formations being more than remarkable. But porterage, fuel, and food, even for coolies, can scarcely be obtained, and only by providing it beforehand, by relays of coolies, sent on in advance by order of some Government official.

The view from Kansam Pass is very grand, looking down the valley over to Lahoul; the mountains on the right are 20,556 and 19,949 feet high, and from the glacier between them the snow is at times blown with cutting severity right across to this Pass. Here I was snowed up two nights and a day; my forty natives, having no shelter, sat in a heap together all night, trying in vain to keep a little fire alight to boil the brick-tea I had given them.

When the snow lies a foot thick no one can travel, as the paths cannot be seen, and one false step might be fatal.

Bourne and Shephard's views in this part of the world are very fine, and I regret I cannot attach copies of all these photographs to these pages that relate to the spot.

We will now presume we have returned to Cheeken and to Prini, where we do not halt, but trot on to Jugget Sookht, a mile or two farther, where we get rid of our coolie porters, pay them, and hire a new set.

There is a neat bungalow here belonging to General Cunnynghame, but in this case there is no tea plantation; being situated at the end of a khud, the cold winds make the winter here very bitter.

A fine large elm tree shades the camping ground, which is very small for tents.

At one side of the camping ground is a small Hindu temple of carved stone in a very perfect condition, but covered with lichens, of which I have made a sketch. There is the peculiarity about it before mentioned, that the mass of carving in front, which is all in one piece of stone, has been shifted about ten inches to the left without further injury to the temple, which is in no wise out of plumb, or the level.

Kell, Bro^s Lith London.

Mr KNOX'S HOUSE, JUGGET SOOKHT.

Another larger wooden temple seems to have been built on the ruins of an older stone one, and numerous altars and blocks of richly-carved stone are found all round. Moorcroft mentions the invasion of Kulu as having been undertaken by the grandfather of Sandsar Chand, and attributes the demolition and injuries to the temples, especially at Bajaura, to his soldiers. This must have been long prior to Runjeet Singh's raids.* The site of the bungalow (which is private and never let, or seldom used) is that of an old fort, or temple. Every year the natives ascend to the top step, which they worship or venerate. There were a few carved stones up there also, but they have been either broken up or built into walls and outhouses, as may be seen.

Behind the wooden temple are the remains of a form, or seat of clayslate, the seat being tenoned through the side standards, which are after the pattern of an old Gothic seat in an English country church. There is part of a similar one below the Tehseel at Sultanpur, but it is not so perfect.

There is another small temple in the village with the Davi enthroned inside, but it has no unusual interest.

Down the khud, and over the bridge, puts us on the road to Nugger Castle. This is now the residence of the Assistant-Commissioner. Moorcroft states this was once the capital of Kulu under another name.

* See Moorcroft, p. 170.

It would be interesting to know the facts how this ancient palace and fort got into the hands of private persons. Government have, however, lately insisted on purchasing it for the Assistant-Commissioner's residence at *his* request, at which no "Naboth" dare complain.

From its elevated position, and what we see of the ancient part, this building must originally have had a very imposing effect, but its glories have long since departed: the first floor has been cut away to make the ground floor higher, and huge *sash* windows placed in the whole height of the two rooms; and a species of Jacob's ladder erected outside, exposed to all weathers, forms the means of access to the upper floors to prevent the necessity of using the original rather imposing entrance and stairs, which one would have thought would answer every purpose; but a wretched Vandalism has converted the whole native palace and fort into a nondescript half tea warehouse, half bungalow, half stable, the cattle being kept in the Zenana at the top.

The view from Nugger is very fine, and at a little distance on the hill below, are the stones erected to the women of the Rajahs who suffered Suttee at their decease.

If we judge from the stones the wives were numerous, and indeed the family, as there are over a hundred, but no inscriptions on any of them.

From Nugger there is a path up to Malauna, and

TEMPLE JUGGET SOOKHT

Page 64.

J. Calvert. Kell Bros Lith. London

DOORWAY OF TEMPLE AT RIWALSIR.

p. 100

LARGER TEMPLE AT JUGGET SOOKHT.

p. 95

J. Calvert.

Kell Brot Lith

by way of Kashole to Manikarn, but it is very precipitous, and few persons attempt it. There is a copper and a lead mine there, but never worked, though the lead is rich in silver. The people of Malauna do not speak the same language as the Kulu people, or any others in India, and it is a question of interest where they could have originally come from. Their village is so isolated, they seldom communicate with the other part or Valley of Kulu, but live almost entirely to themselves.

Our best road now is to return by crossing the river to Dobie, and it is only a "long" march (13 miles) to Sultanpur. From here we can ascend to Bijli, and down the other side to Chamaun, and next day along Parbutti Valley; but it will be better, if we are returning by the Bubu Pass to Kangra or Cashmere hereafter, to go from Sultanpur to Shumshee, crossing the river there by ferry to Buin camping ground. Here we again enter "Vazeeri Rupi."

There is a path over Sultanpur Bridge and along the side of Bijli, but it is not a good one to ride or even walk; it brings you to Jia at the foot of Bijli, from whence you cross the new bridge to the camping ground at Buin.

Few Europeans have ever been in the village of Buin, but the camping ground under the trees on the river side is very delightful, except for the noise of the rushing stream.

The mountain above "Kot Kandi" is very rich in

mineral, principally copper, which shows in numerous places, as also manganese and iron, and on the other side sulphur is found.

Previous to turning the corner of the Parbutti River, on the right hand of the road and a little above the foot of the hill, may be distinctly seen a huge mass of a copper lode covered with the brilliant green exudation, which ordinarily follows long exposure of rocks containing copper ore.

I have seen such stains a mile long in South Africa. Although copper may be found in several places up the mountain side, yet there can be no doubt, on comparing them, this piece of rock came from a huge lode high up over the top of that mountain at the back of the village of Saond, but by what means it got into its present position is a problem indeed, as no volcanic action has been at work there to have hurled it such a distance over the ridge; had it merely been removed down a slope we could have imagined the ice and snow to have been the means, as we can see every day in the mountains above during the snow.

The village at the foot of Bijli Mountain across the Parbutti River, to the left, is Jia, the former capital of Kulu; it was here the remains of the late Rae were brought for cremation. At one time there was an interesting temple there, but I hear the last stone was lately used to build a new bridge with here. The scenery from the turn of the road round this corner is very picturesque, and the road has been greatly improved of late. On reaching the highest part the road is covered with very fine specimens of ripple-marked, altered sandstone, almost purely white. Some distance farther the road nears the stream, where some large rocks are in the centre. One of these fell only three years ago from the higher part of the mountain above south, making fearful devastation in its course, carrying away the entire road it fell on.

At the corner is rather a *cranky* bit of road cut in the solid rock, and not a desirable place to ride over, as well as very awkward for a heavy dholie. The road is better when you get to the bridge over the Chiol Khud. Up here, again, the copper shows very strong, but has never been mined or worked on : and farther on, near Barogi village, the mountain is said to be all rock salt. The road up the khud is rather rough and not at all tempting.

The road now begins to ascend a very steep incline, but on the top it is better : from either place you can see the winding road in advance cut into the solid rock, and overhanging at the distant corner we have to pass round shortly after, you have to step over another copper lode which shows out in the road and below.

The road now becomes narrow for a little, but quite safe, being cut in the perpendicular rock, though some people fear to look down upon the foaming stream rushing far below. There is something very interesting in those pretty farm-houses on the other side: their very isolation seems to have a charm, yet it must be a climb to get at them or away from them, and the happy owner must have learnt to concentrate all his wants into the few necessaries he can obtain there without going daily to "the bazaar."

We now reach a cool and welcome spring and shady trees. This place is called Gula Pani, and though the water is good, the place is always filthy from the cattle watering there. In the hill above is a lead and silver vein, which no doubt, if traced, would prove larger farther on.

A little farther on, round the corner, and the worst part of the road, is one of the prettiest sights in all Kulu: on a projecting ridge of clayslate stands the old fort of Chong on the south side, many hundred feet nearly perpendicular above the bed of the stream; but the other side is a gradual cultivated slope. It must be about 2000 feet above the river, and will be seen in a different height a mile or two farther on. A lady is said to have fallen from the top of this, and yet to have lived; it must certainly depend on which side of the mountain she fell. Above the village of Chong, which has a nice camping ground, but is a bad place for supplies, is the richest silver mine in the valley, near Chitrani. It was built up to hide it from the Sikhs, and has not yet been re-worked. Copper is also reported here in its native state—not as a sulphuret.

Kell Bro^s Lith.

CHONG FORT – PARBUTTI VALLEY – CHAMAUN OPPOSITE.

The houses in the forest, with their red roofs, look very picturesque, and the ridge on which the old fort stands will be seen to run up the whole side of the valley, and is very distinctly seen from the opposite side.

From here the large tree on the opposite ridge can be see again as a landmark.

The road farther on, after one little bad piece, is very good, and you can canter along a few miles with comfort, but do not forget to turn round to look at Chong from the different positions. A sudden turn on the bared clayslate rock brings you to "Ramunkote," where is a neat-cut temple and fountain of beautiful water; the road beyond is disgustingly narrow, through walls of loose stone, till a sudden turn brings you to the top of a steep descent. This in wet weather is dangerously slippery; the adjacent woods abound with game, especially partridge and chikor. Another turn to the right brings you into Shatghur, the water from which is of excellent purity and clearness, that every stone in its bed can be distinctly seen at all times. Here also are more lodes of copper hitherto unworked. Crossing the bridge the new road leads up a steep, after which a mile of level road leads to a nice spring, under some shady trees, where tiffin is acceptable. The rocks here are worthy of observation, and there is no hiding that serious-looking flight of steps in the solid rock by which you have to ascend over 200 feet.

This pinky white or peachy coloured metamorphic sandstone is very crystalline, and is similar to the celebrated Kansas stone, of which the Americans make their noted whetstones, which sell at a great price.

At the summit the road betters again, and an easy ride brings us to a sharp corner; before turning this, let us step a few paces to the left under the tree on this projecting point. What a lovely sight is here! Over the river on the left is the village of Choki, and at the back the entrance of the Malauna Khud, approachable by a bridge far below. On the right among the clump of walnut trees is Jerri, the camping ground being under the trees. Above are immense forests, which supply the railways with sleepers by the thousand; the trees are felled and cut into lengths here, each log over nine feet, with the date of the year it was felled; these are all slid down the mountain side into the river, where they take their chance till they reach the wide but shallow water of Nadoun, where they are stopped and placed in the Government depôt; but a large number are stolen, they say, in their transit down to there. The villages to the right are Mateara, Buhar, and others above the Kanor Khud, where the silver mines are, and up the valley we see part of our road to the holy hot springs at Manikarn.

At Jerri you get supplies and bearers, if needed, Manikarn being the next stage.

Kell Bros. Lith.

CHONG FROM THE NORTH — BIJLI TEMPLE (8,076 FT.) OPPOSITE.

The road from Jerri for about a mile abounds in mineral veins—silver, lead, and copper having been dug out in many places. On reaching Kanor Khud, about a mile down on the right-hand side, there are many old workings about the bed of the river, but the rich silver mines are up this khud; here was the only mine which the natives disclosed to the Sikhs when they occupied the country, and which they blew up the entrance to on leaving. Some of the ore from this mine is said to have produced 1 in 16 parts of silver.

What was taken out by myself from the rubbish at the entrance was kindly assayed by Dr. Oldham, and produced "99 ounces of silver, a large percentage of copper, and some gold."

So entirely has the existence of silver in this country been forgotten, that we find the following in Cunnynghame's Ladak:—"The sands of the Indus have long been celebrated for the production of gold. Pliny says: '*Fertilisiru sunt auri Dardœ*,' and this is the case to the present day, for the sands of the Indus in the Dardœ country are said to be more prolific than those of any part of the river (Lib. vi., c. 19). The conclusion of the passage is curious and suggestive: 'Setœ vero argenti,' that is, the country of the Dardœ produced most gold, but that of the Setœ most silver."

"As we know," remarks Major Cunnynghame (p. 232), "that *silver is not found in India*, the Setœ can be no other than the seths or bankers, in whose hands the wealth of India has been for ages."

Surely Major C. must have heard of Vezeeri Rupi, "the silver country of the Vazeers," in Kulu, covering 677 miles, and abounding in silver ores; for such an authority to say there is *no silver in India* is astonishing.

When ascending this khud some distance up, my attention was attracted by an appearance of mineral indication in the rock above. Determined to examine the spot more closely, I attempted to cross the stream to the opposite bank, which was nearly perpendicular, but my foot slipped, and to save myself from falling into the stream I seized the root of a fig-tree growing in the perpendicular rock close at hand, where the soil gave way, and with the portion of the root came out, to my amazement, a large lode of rich silver lead as thick as my leg.

This led to further discoveries of other rich veins, and I afterwards heard there is a rich mine about here, but it was planted over to hide it from the Sikhs. There is also a lode of "native copper" up this khud. Indeed the number of veins and indications of mineral wealth about here is beyond credence, and days and days may be spent in the discovery and collecting specimens: but this is not permitted.

The view from the miners' camp, on the spur of the hill, amply repays for the ascent, especially the

Kell Bro^s. Lith.

SILVER MINE, KANOR KHUD AND VILLAGE OF CHOKI _ PARBUTTI VALLEY.

village of Choki and the Krunchall Mountain we saw from Sultanpur at the other side.

The view from the "camp" forms one of the engravings. On the steppes of the mountain opposite are extensive pine forests, which at a distance only exhibit a dark shade, but are thick groves. The prominent tree on the extreme right is a juniper cedar of great age and beauty. The silver mine is close to the tree on the left, in the foreground, and the village of Mateara is above.

This is a favourite place for the monkeys to gambol about daily.

Below the road and farther on are dozens more lodes and indication of copper and silver, lead, &c. Numerous entrances may be seen below, but most of them fallen in, or purposely filled up and planted over with thorns.

There is an apparent "working" on the other side of the stream—not easily accessible. On turning up to the right a peculiar formation diverts the road—a slip of decomposed clayslate spoils the road, and we descend over the steps of metamorphic sandstone down towards the bed of the river. Here a large amount of timber has been cut, but the water is too shallow to carry it down. In the quartzose rock about here, and indeed for miles on, is much emerald-green oxide of chrome, which looks very beautiful, but is hard to detach; also micaceous iron, which has been taken for black-lead. The road continues very picturesque till we come to Kasole, up which khud is another mine, and here we cross the "Parbutti" by a long wooden bridge.

I once passed this bridge and looked back for a friend who was travelling with me, but for some time could not see anything of him. After I had got some distance I turned back and saw him crossing the bridge *on his hands and knees,*—his long beard hanging down gave him more the appearance of a goat than a human being. A few days' chaff soon cured him of his fears, however, and he now crosses on his feet only. About three miles' pleasant walk brings us to Manikarn, the very *stink* of which is considered sacred, and "one journey here in a life ensures admittance to heaven."

There is a great deal in the idea of this, if one could only believe it as sincerely as thousands of natives do. What can be their idea of heaven, if such is the road to it?

There is a temple at Manikarn said to be 1800 years old, where the debris from the mountain above and other causes have raised the land around it so much that the natives fancy the temple has sunk from its extreme age—like many of the cathedrals in England, especially York Minster. The digging of numberless graves round had so raised the churchyard many feet, that the Minster seems to have sunk, and it is quite common to see them entered by steps down.

Kell Bros Lith

STONE HOUSE AT MANIKARN_PARBUTTI VALLEY.

The house of one of the headmen lately built there is the prettiest specimen of Kulu building extant, every stone is "dressed," and is said to have been dug from the ruin of an ancient temple there, and the carving of the woodwork is really most commendable. The lower part is used as a granary, and the upper part a nice dwelling.

The boiling water rises from the ground, or in some places gushes out from a crevice in the metamorphic rocks which rise perpendicular many hundred feet above, as in the Andes, while the hot puddles and refuse streams astonish the incautious *dog* who "puts his foot in it."

Beyond Manikarn, about three miles, at Uchiech, are the celebrated Manikarn "Silver Mines," and again at Pulga—which is almost as far as any European has gone in that almost uninhabited land, but there is no reason why there should not be boundless sources of wealth farther west.

Some ore from the silver mines at Uchiech was exhibited in the Lahore Museum, 1863; but it appears there are several lodes about Manikarn, galena, arsenical and iron pyrites; but the access is rather precipitous for natives to incline to reach them, though they have long been known, and are prominently defined in the trigonometrical survey maps of India.

One of the Manikarn mines is galena, another is principally arsenical pyrites. Dr. Stolitska gave me an uninviting description of his visit to one of them, being let down by a rope round his waist, &c. It seems a wonder to me the learned geologist should have taken so much pains to see this, and yet to have literally walked over a dozen others, and never noted them. He informed me, however, that the weather was so bad during his excursion there, that he had little or no opportunity of seeing the country fairly. This was a great pity, as a gentleman of his known ability would have been able to give more information than I possibly can.

There are one or two stone baths at Manikarn supplied with the "native liquor"; and, judging from the appearance of the many who enter after their pilgrimage of many weeks' travel, I should say it was rather a desideratum. But there are no means of changing the water, and the smell became so very *strong* that I packed up my ores from the mine, and was rather glad to leave Manikarn, especially as the headman assured me I was "certain to go to heaven now" for having visited the Holy Baths—which is rather consolatory, considering the many opportunities I have had of breaking my neck since.

"According to the legend, the goddess Parbati having laid her jewels upon the bank whilst she was bathing with Mahadeva in the river, her ear-rings (Manikarnika) were stolen and carried off to Patala, the regions below the earth, by the serpent Sesha.

"At the probable consequences of the Mahadeva's

wrath the gods discovered the thief, and urgently pressed the Naga to restore the plunder. Sesha refused, claiming the ear-rings as his own property, but as he snorted with indignation the subject of dispute issued from his nostrils, in which it had been concealed, and flew back to the goddess.

"Through the openings made by its passage to the surface of the earth, boiled water has ever since continued to flow."

I think I copied this from Moorcroft; anyhow there can be no doubt it's all *true*.

The way back from Manikarn can be varied by going to Jerri again, and down the steps to Shatghur; but after crossing the bridge, keep the bank of the river to the right, instead of going up the slippery hill to the left. After passing some more mineral lodes in the rocks, continue *down* the stream,—the road being all comparatively level, till you come out below the foot of Chong, where there is another of those picturesque bridges. At certain seasons you can "camp out" here pleasantly under large walnut trees before crossing the bridge. On the opposite side, also up the steep ascent, is another silver-lead lode, but difficult of access. The road now is a continual rise for some hours of 4000 feet. There is a very small resting ground at Chamoun, from whence you get a beautiful view of Chong Fort and all the road we passed going up the Parbutti.

From Chamoun the road is partly through a forest,

where *if it be wet* the clay is inconceivably inconvenient to climb; and, whatever the inclination may be, the probability is you will leave *one* boot behind. There is another shorter road, under that large tree at the summit, by the large tree at Kot Kassie, instead of going up to Bijli, but the Bijli is the easier route, and can be *done* on horse most if not all of the way. On the summit of Bijli there is a temple to the goddess of lightning, and ponds of water to supply the cattle. The view from here up the Maol Khud and down the Kulu Valley, and of all the mountains round, amply repays for any exertion in reaching the top.

The descent is easy, the road being safe all the way; and the distance from Chamoun to Sultanpur about five hours' walk; this finds us again at Sultanpur Rest-house.

FROM KULU TO KANGRA.

The route back by the Bubu Pass, although entailing a long climb the second day, is nevertheless a favourite trip, the scenery being more than interesting all the way to the plains, and the road beyond Kangra in particular a good cart-road; there is also the convenience of rest-houses at every stage. The river is called the "Sivbarry."

The first stage up the Sultanpur or Sivbarry Khud, is a most agreeable walk, the road being fair all the way to Karowne, which I measured as being 6384 feet, or about 2300 above Sultanpur. There is a large slate quarry over the river about three miles up, if you can call it slate from being so commonly used throughout the valley to "slate" houses, it being a garnetiferous strongly micaceous schist.

These slates are sold in quantities at Sultanpur.

The rest-house at Karowne is pleasant if in repair; from it may be seen the stone tower of "Kot Kassie" on the Bijli ridge, which is not visible from Sultanpur, and the large tree before mentioned as being so conspicuous.

This is the last British rest-house; there is also a very neat native serai below it. We now leave for Bubu Pass, Mundi territory.

Leaving this we follow the stream and continue gradually to rise, soon getting into an eternal zig-zag among the fine forest of trees which prove a grateful shade; while the ferns, which are in abundance and great variety, begin now to be conspicuous all the way.

The occasional views from here looking back are transitory but beautiful, for the clouds of mist flit by vexatiously; just as you get a lovely view, and begin to appreciate how lovely such a village is on the summit of such a hill, a cloud passes over it, and it gradually disappears.

The cutting at the top is always wet, there being a fine spring of water, which however damages the road seriously; there is also a fine peachy "flukan lode, which is assuredly metallic below—I should say copper.

If the weather is fine, the view from the summit is very grand on both sides, but you may wait for hours to get a glimpse through the flitting clouds, that seem determined to drench you through, or hasten you down the other side, which being in Mundi territory, is generally in a very bad condition, being cut up by the streams from above.

The Rajah of Mundi has, however, spent enormous sums of money to make and keep these roads passable.

The descent is rough and tedious, and it seems a great pity a tunnel was not cut some two thousand feet below the pass, and so much distance and labour saved.

Budwanee is the next stage, and a nice bungalow it is, though supplies are usually scarce here. The house cannot be seen till you turn up from the precipitous road and round the corner; its position is then found commanding a splendid view, including two miles of the next road gradually ascending the other side; the slate on this bungalow was all brought from near Palumpore, I am told. I was very glad to spend a few days here, especially as there had been heavy rains, and the road was very much damaged indeed,—nearly impassable. This is probably the worst bit in the whole journey; in some places the road has entirely slipped down, leaving about six inches, and the rock above overhanging. We managed, however, dholie and horse and all, to get over it safe, and soon reached the cutting or pass at the top of the opposite rise,—the rock being a decomposed black slate, no doubt repaired since then, as Lord Mayo passed through, November, 1871.

The road then becomes wide and pretty level, but incessantly winding in and out; there is a fine view also, if not cloudy, as you jog along under the shady trees; the rock is mostly gneiss decomposed and sandstone shale, the mountains being very steep, and the forests of timbers all useless for want of carriage.

Suddenly, but by no means too soon, Jitringee Rest-house comes in sight: this is rather a damp, uncomfortable house, and was lately much out of repair. I found it 5997 feet above sea level, and there is a very fine view from here of the lower country, when the weather is fair.

There is a path from the back of this place that leads to Mundi, and is used by those going to Kulu *viâ* "Rupereri" or Bajara Khud, when the Bubu is closed by snow, which is the case from November to March.

From here the descent becomes sudden and continuous for some time, winding through the forest, when you emerge on a more level road that still winds in and out round the spurs of the mountains,

G 2

crossing streams which have no bridges, and are sometimes deep.

The first one, which is just past the village of "Gamel," surprises you by the pink colour of the water, which is caused by its running from a mine of salt in a decomposed calcareous sandstone. This mine is not at present worked, the rubbish having accumulated so extensively; but there are other similar salt mines in Mundi that bring the Rajah several lacs of rupees revenue annually.

A little farther on there is another torrent to cross, but not salt. It is much to be regretted this and several others are not bridged, being at times dangerous to ford.

We now pass over a gentle rise whereon is an old small Hindu temple, and on the right hand we get a sight of Harabagh, a bungalow presented by the Rajah of Mundi to his former tutor, Mr. Clarke, but not always occupied. Another small stream is forded, but we have yet still another, the bridge over which has been carried away, and a rope and basket has been rigged up for the dâk runner, in case the river is in flood, for one man has already been drowned trying to pass. There are usually extra men there waiting to earn a few pice, and we put the dholie on the men's heads, but the water is up to their armpits, and the horse must swim. This is not always the case, but there is no place on the whole route where a bridge is more required, and by diverting the road a little lower down the stream, a plank or two would effect a crossing both short and safe: on rising up the incline we now see the nice rest-house at Dhailoo. This is a new and comfortable bungalow in a delightful spot, and offering a grand view of the Kangra Valley. Above the bungalow are the remains of a large fort and palace, which are only approachable from the other side. It is called Curunpore, and is said to have been the residence of the ancient Rajahs of Mundi, "being 1700 years old." Here was also the original capital of Mundi territory till removed to the more retired place where it is now. The ruin is very interesting, but so overgrown with jungle inside, that I found it impossible to get over it even to take the ground plan.

Here I had the misfortune to break my thermometer, so could not ascertain the height we were at.

Next journey we pass through the tea plantation belonging to the Rajah of Mundi. We pass also several old castles, some of very great extent, but they are out of the road, though I have no doubt well worth examination, as they are all constructed in a superior manner to anything erected in our days. It is plain there was no "Public Works Department" (the disgrace of India) in the days they were built.

From the top of a hill, which commands a view of all the valley of Kangra, we descend rapidly to the interesting village of Bijnath. Here are some elaborately carved old Hindu temples, and actually a post-office! The village is in a dense mass of vegetation, and is muddy and damp. Monkeys congregate in hundreds, and seem much *interested in the arrival of strangers.* The rest-house is capacious, but badly built and worse cared for. The view of the river below and the mountains above would make a good photograph, but better painting; it is full of detail, with an elegant temple by the river side in the left foreground. Down the steep bank and over a good stone bridge, we soon get on the plains and pass through repeated tea plantations on the long spurs of the hill, and during rainy weather the descent of these repeated ridges is almost dangerous, the soil being a greasy red clay. A small but inconvenient stream, which is not bridged, runs across the approach to Palumpore. Palumpore is in fact a nice *street* on the spur of a hill; the Rajah of Mundi has built a school there, and the Government a good dâk bungalow: there is a common bazaar and the beginning of a stone church. The European inhabitants being limited to two or three families of tea planters at a distance, the chaplain from Dhurumsala will attend occasionally to perform service. There is a fair held here every November, which, but for some *croquet playing*, is said to be a failure; the ground undulates all round, and is covered with fir trees, under which the Yarkandees and others visiting the fair can camp, and the whole is no doubt very picturesque. There are a few shawl weavers in the bazaar, but it appeared to me the place was a failure.

It lacks sadly a large Maidan like Kulu, and its approaches want improving and bridging. If the roads were bettered, bridges built, and ridges tunnelled, Kulu would be a much better market than Palumpore.

To Dhurumsala is a double stage, there being a rest-house at Dadh, which is about half way or more.

Dhurumsala is a very scattered and certainly a *hill* station, for the post-office and church are miles apart from each other, and the dâk bungalow, which is, or I hope only *was*, the most dilapidated, dirty, leaky, smelling place I have yet seen in India under the name, is several miles from both.

The Commissioner's house is 9205 feet above sea level, 3106 feet above the dâk bungalow.

To Kangra, which is worth looking at, especially the splendid old fort, and on to the plains, is a route scarcely worth describing, being so well known; the road is good all the way for horses, camels, carts, or almost a buggy, but by dholie you may be at Hosheyarpore in a few hours, and two hours and a half after in the train for Calcutta or Lahore.

Mr. G. Barnes, in his settlement report, says of Kangra Valley: "I know no spot in the Himalayas which for beauty or grandeur can compete with the Kangra Valley and these overshadowing hills.

"No scenery presents such sublime and delightful

contrasts. Below lies the plain, a picture of rural loveliness and repose. The surface is covered with the richest cultivation, irrigated by streams which descend from perennial snows, and interspersed with homesteads buried in the midst of groves and fruit trees. Turning from this scene of peaceful beauty the stern and majestic hills confront us.

"Their sides are furrowed with precipitous water-courses, forests of oak clothe their flanks, and higher up give place to gloomy and funeral pines. Above all are wastes of snow, on pyramidal masses of granite too perpendicular for the snow to rest upon."

To this Major Paske, in his late memorandum, adds:—"Beautiful as is the Kangra Valley, thus so well described, it is even surpassed by the loveliness of the scenery in the Kooloo Valley, one of the sub-divisions of the district."

I am at a loss to understand why the Government draw the attention of settlers so strenuously to Kangra and Kulu, as I believe there is no possibility of anyone, even of moderate influence, obtaining land in either place; and as to tea, as yet only one plantation makes enough to pay the delectable—Income-tax.

The productions of Kulu are Indian corn, wheat, barley, peas, beans, rapeseed, millet, cotton, tobacco, great quantities of which are exported, poppy, opium (this pays no duty), endless varieties of rice and very fine potatoes; there is some tea, but the "agent" informed me that it does not succeed in Kulu, and his attention is now directed to purchasing up every bit of land he can for his employers, who already have the entire monopoly to themselves, and renting it out to the natives for half the crops.

The cultivation in Kulu depends mainly upon irrigation; this is supplied from the mountain streams direct, or raised from them by the many methods used throughout India.

The bed of the entire valley is a loose conglomerate, through which the water percolates from the surface, leaving it hard and dry, thus rendering irrigation absolutely necessary.

The numerous mills for grinding corn are ingenious and effective, though constructed in the rudest manner possible; they are turbines. Near the lower end of an axle which is fixed so as to revolve upright, are fixed eight or ten fans of wood, at an angle of 45° with the axle. To the top of this axle is fixed the upper millstone. A stream of water is then conducted so as to fall at an angle on the fans of the wheel which turns the mill. With but a moderate stream the whole power of the water is made effective. No iron is used in any part, so that the owner can easily keep it in repair. Hundreds of these mills cover the valley, and the miller is paid by taking a share of the grain brought to be ground.

Fruit abounds in Kulu; the walnuts being very fine. Apricots and peaches grow for miles on each side of the road and in every garden and hedge, but are not cultivated, and for the most part plucked and eaten by the youthful population long before they are ripe, thus giving work to the native doctor at the Dispensary, or conducing to lessen the rising population. Peas, strawberries, raspberries, french beans, artichokes of both kinds, cauliflowers, &c., thrive, and there are wild strawberries in many places, of a small size but pleasant flavour. Grapes are found here and there, but are not properly attended to, or might, I am sure, be made profitable. There is a small blue wild plum grows in great abundance in summer, and tempts the bears down during the daytime.

The potatoes are regularly cultivated by the natives, and are very fine. They are sold at the rate of a maund for a rupee cash, but at a higher rate in bartering.

Figs, citrons, limes, and grape-fruits thrive in abundance, and rot on the ground for want of gathering.

The tops of the mountains which incline to the north are covered with "deodar," or pitch-pines, and other inferior kinds of fir; they nowhere favour the south aspect. Below are elms of fine proportions, and plenty of oak. The oaks are mostly kept pollarded, the foliage being cut off every winter as food for goats and sheep, and are therefore stinted in growth.

Some Government official was handsomely rewarded for finding a tree of box in Kulu, yet it may be seen lying about the farmyards as not unusually scarce or valuable; for it would not pay to transport it to the plains.

I found yew trees and juniper cedars (but got no reward). There is a fine wild plum tree which works up into handsome furniture. I also discovered during my sojourn there the following metallic ores and minerals:—Gold; the ores of silver, lead, copper, and iron in abundance; bismuth, manganese, and tin. There is also antimony, but not in so large a lode as at Shigri in Lahoul.

Iron is smelted and worked by the natives in large quantities in the neighbouring States, and at the annual fair brought to Kulu. A favourite article is a saucepan beaten out of solid iron; they also manufacture large boilers for sugar, &c.; and I am informed the secret of preparing the fine steel for swords, &c., is the use of charcoal made from the root of a euphorbia which bears a pod of silken fibre and is common throughout India, and the manufacture being conducted with stone hammers and anvil.

The iron is smelted with limestone flux and the use of a goat-skin bellows.

Copper ore is smelted without coal or wood in some places. This is effected by breaking the ore up fine and mixing it with cakes of gobar (or cattle dung), which, being placed in a heap and fired, the copper ore runs out at the bottom.

The minerals are as follows:—Rock crystal, tourmalin, kyanite, hornblende, green oxide of chrome, micaceous iron, spathic iron, carbonate of iron, or siderose, mispikel, or arsenical pyrites, pyrolusite, galena, stibnite, kermesite, or red antimony (a very rare mineral), cervantite, carbonate of lime, zincblende, copper pyrites, sulphate of copper, or bluestone, carbonate of baryta, feldspar, mica, serpentine, with thin seams of white, asbestus, salt, limestones, garnets, sapphires, rubies, sulphur, gypsum, borax, and epidote.

There is much gypsum and borax in Spiti also and Lahoul, from whence large quantities are brought down on mules to the plains, the latter selling at about Rs. 6 per maund (equal to 12*s.* for 80 lbs.). It is purified by boiling and crystallizing at the bazaar Sultanpur. From gypsum the plaster of Paris is made. The finest rock crystal is useful for making into optical glasses, like "Brazilian pebbles," and when "brilliant cut" have been mistaken for diamonds. Quantities of good-sized crystals have been found on the north side of Kanor Khud, opposite the Silver Mine.

The rocks comprise a coarse feldspathic gneiss, metamorphic sandstones, clayslate, sandstone shales, limestone rocks of great variety, limestone conglomerates and micaceous sandstones, shales, schists, and slates, and good building sandstone.

The mine in Shigri is leased for twenty years from

Keil, Bro^s. lith.

VILLAGE OF CHATE ON ROAD TO KULU FROM SIMLA.

Government; the mineral rights of Vazeeri Rupi, which covers 677 square miles and has a population of between three and four thousand, do not belong to Government, but are private property. It is proposed to raise a company to work the whole.

Rewards are given for the bodies of all bears, leopards, and other destructive wild animals, which are then skinned and the skins sold to travellers, or residents by the Tehseeldar at Sultanpur; but there is sometimes a great trouble to get a sight of them, and they remain locked up in an outhouse by dozens until they are entirely eaten up by vermin.

Sheep are scarce, but sold at Rs. 2 8 annas, or 4*s.* to 8*s.* each, according to size, and the price fixed by Assistant-Commissioner; poultry 4 or 5 for a rupee, and eggs 30 for a rupee, but the fixed price is 16 for a rupee, which is exorbitant, being 1½*d.* each.

The temperature of Kulu is moderate, but of course varies according to the part of the valley you reside in.

Sultanpur is more open than Dobie or Manali, but farther north than Bajara, where I have known the glass at 100° Fahr. in verandah the day before the rains commenced, invariably the hottest time in India. In the winter I never saw it below 32°. The snow never lies on the ground after 7 or 8 A.M., and the air is clear and bracing.

At Sultanpur I never found it hotter than 96° inside the tent and 82° inside the rest-house in summer, or below 30° in winter.

During March the weather is very windy and wet. The wind is also very severe just before the rainy season, but on the whole the climate is much like the South of England, and very healthy.

There is a peculiarity in the currency at Kulu that is not recognized in the plains. The natives will not take British copper money; the reason is this: sixteen British copper annas are not worth more than about twelve annas of silver, or eighteen-pence instead of two shillings. I could not ascertain where the copper money they use was coined, but it is half the diameter and three times the thickness; three usually count for an anna, or forty-eight for a silver rupee; but the price varies continually according to the value of copper in the market, sheet copper there being sold at 112*l*. to 120*l*. per ton.

The Bunyahs here as elsewhere deal in change, and charge for changing copper to silver or silver to copper alike.

There is a gold yarkand piece often for sale in Kulu; the value in gold is ten shillings English, but they ask six rupees for them.

APPENDIX.

ROUTES TO KULU FROM THE PLAINS.

DIRECT route from the railway at Umballa is only sixteen marches or less, but has the disadvantage of being rough and only fit for coolies to travel; besides which, it passes principally through the independent territories of Belaspore, Suket, and Mundi, there being few if any resting-places for Europeans.

Route direct from Umballa to Kulu :—

UMBALLA.—1. 2. Chut Bunnor. 3. 4. Kerull. 5. Keralee. 6. Ropur. 7. Kunolee. 8. Mongowar. 9. Kondloo. 10. Satghur. 11. Belaspore. 12. Dheir. 13. Sukyt or Suket. 14. Mundi. 15. Komand. 16. Bajara, Kulu Valley.

The Mail route to Kulu from Jullunder on the Lahore and Delhi Railway is as follows:—

From Jullunder to Hosheyarpore, 20 miles.—This is usually performed in about two hours by horse dâk.

From Hosheyarpore to Gugrate, 15½ miles on a good cart-road.—There is a serai or rest-house at Nari Pass, but it is better to go on to Gugrate, where the accommodation is excellent, and supplies can be had. The view of the Lower Snowy Himalayahs from here is very interesting, and in the valley in front may be found any amount of black buck.

From Gugrate to Purwain, 13 miles.—After a little rough road crossing the river bed the road winds through the forest, eventually reaching a very nice rest-house—or rather dâk bungalow, for here you can get supplies—on the summit of small hill, from whence the view is fine.

From Purwain to Deyrah, 15 miles.—This is a long winding route, and eventually leads to a large river, which has to be crossed in flats kept for hire, the rest-house being very near the other side.

From Deyrah to Ranetalah, 10 miles.—A bad rest-house, with no attendance. It is better to go on a double march.

From Ranetalah to Kangra, 11 miles, where there is a fine dâk bungalow on a very high eminence commanding a view of all the country round.—The view of the ancient and formidable Castle and Fort

Kell. Broˢ. Lith.

NEAR RUSALA.

of Kangra, as seen when approaching from the opposite side of the river, is exceedingly grand.

From Kangra to Dhurumsala, 12 miles, is a good road till you approach the range.—There is a dâk bungalow here, but the principal houses are scattered over the hills. From here passengers go to Dalhousie and Chumba, and on to Cashmere.

From Dhurumsala to Palumpore, 19 miles.—Since I passed I believe there is a half-stage over the river at Dadh, but it is very small. At Palumpore is a handsome dâk bungalow.

From Palumpore to Byjnath, 10 miles.—Large rest-house.

From Byjnath to Dhailoo, in Mundi, 10 miles.—A beautifully clean rest-house in a lovely spot.

From Dhailoo to Jitringee, 12 miles.—This road cannot be used by carts on account of the many streams. There is a rest-house, but it is rather damp. From here the road turns to Mundi city. When the Bubu Pass is closed in winter it is three stages.

From Jitringee to Budwanee, 15 miles.—A long winding road under the pleasant shade of trees, and very level all the way till we approach the pleasant newly-built bungalow, which may be seen miles off from this side.

From Budwanee to Karowne, 12 miles.—A British rest-house in Kulu.

From Karowne to Sultanpur, the capital of Kulu, 10 miles.—Kulu Valley.

The first six of the above marches can be performed in a day and night by Palkie Dak.

At most of the stages in this route where out of British control the porters or coolies are engaged through a head man, who receives a portion of the money himself for the trouble of collecting them, and the traveller pays them the remainder. The usual charge is 3 annas per 10-mile stage.

Kulu Valley is also ten marches north of Simla, and this route is often made part of the route to Cashmere, but there are only a few rest-houses between Simla and Kulu, so that a tent is requisite.

The stages are as follows:—1. Simla to Fagu, 12 miles. 2. Fagu to Theog, 8 miles. 3. Theog to Narkundah, 10 miles. 4. Narkundah to Dilachee ("a hard grind"), 16 miles. 5. Dilachee to Choie, 8 miles. 6. Choie to Kote, 11 miles. 7. Kote to Jerhee, 12 miles. 8. Jerhee to Plach, 8 miles; rest-house. 9. Plach to Largi, 12 miles; rest-house. 10. Largi to Bajaura in Kulu, 13 miles; good rest-house.

There is a driving road from Umballa to Simla.

There is another route to Kulu, which, however, is not frequently used by Europeans, chiefly because there are few if any rest-houses on the line, and parts of the road are so rough and precipitous that mules cannot go with luggage all the way, though it is somewhat shorter, and never closed by snow.

THE CHATA RIVER BETWEEN SIMLA AND KULU.

The route is as follows:—Jullunder to Hosheyarpore, Hosheyarpore to Gugrate. From here we cross the valley and river bed, which abounds with black buck, in nearly a northerly direction, passing through the pleasant gardens of Umb, a private snuggery of the Great Mogul. From there, after enjoying some luscious fruit, presented by the natives in charge, we followed the bed of a long, winding, deep nullah, whose perpendicular sides were from 50 to 100 feet high, of conglomerate, and in many places infested with monkeys.

The ascent at the end was severe and very sudden, but the view from the ridge at the top was extensive.

The descent at the other side was as steep, but through a pleasant wood, and at the bottom in the valley we encamped near an ancient bazaar, called Kulohule. Around here we saw plenty of pheasants and chikor, and got supplies, but it is a filthy place, and full of dirty people.

From Kulohule the road is very picturesque all the way to the southern bank of the Beas River, which comes on the view suddenly as we surmount an elevated ridge. The long-haired goats I met about here attracted my attention, partly by their silken coats and partly from the beautiful and graceful curve of their horns.

Close to the bank of the river, but above it, shaded by a cooling tope of trees, is a well-built stone temple, the carvings on which are finely executed, and, for a wonder, scarcely injured. In the centre of the floor is a four-headed figure, as far down as the shoulders, and larger than life, each face opposite an entrance, so that only three faces can be seen at once, as intended. The spandrils of the entrance—for there are no doors—are filled up by neat carvings of a man riding a swan,* and above is a figure playing on a "banjo." We stayed here to tiffin, and then marched on about three miles to Nadaon, and here we encamped under a tree below the town. Here they wash for gold, the river being shallow and wide, but free from large rocks. Fine pebbles, onyx, and jasper may be picked up here. It is also the depôt for the timber cut and floated down by Government from Kulu.

Nadaon is about 19 miles from the next stage, which has the convenience of a rest-house, and is called Humeerpore. From here we cross a by-road to Simla, merely a bridle path, and crossing a bold stream, we encamped north of it at Kullore.

From Kullore we descended very gradually to a river, where our mules stumbled, and wetted all our luggage and valuable books. The Ayah also came to grief by falling down a khud, but eventually we got a fine camping ground under the trees, part way up the hill at Gopalpore.

Gopalpore is "Thanna" of the maps. The ascent here is great and precipitous, there being four-tenths

* The swan is the usual vehicle of Brahma, the creator of the universe.

Kell Broˢ Lith.

KOT KANDI & VILLAGE OF DIYAR FROM RUPARARI KHUD.

of an inch difference in the barometer on the summit. It puzzled me how the men carried the ladies' dholie and all our luggage up this path, for we had to leave mules now for human labour.

On these mountains are large lakes of fish and plenty of pheasant shooting.

The descent increases steepness, and becomes very abrupt as soon as we approach the Holy Valley and Lake of Riwalsir. Here is a "sacred lake" and "moving island," and several beautifully-carved temples near the bank. There are also wide stone steps and baths for women, enclosed on the banks by a carved stone screen. The fishes come in millions to be fed by the hundreds of pilgrims who come here for thousands of miles distance. Two finely-carved stone bulls ornament the village, and several richly-carved stone temples, similar and in some parts alike the temple we visited before coming to Nadaon.

We have now entered the Rajah of Mundi's territory.

From Riwalsir we ascend out of the natural basin, and follow an interesting but rough road to Mundi city. The last mile had been almost carried away, and we had to cross the river close to Mundi by torchlight, which, though fearful with its rush and roar at night, was barely two feet deep in any part.

At Mundi camping ground we found the Rajah had kindly prepared two suits of handsome tents for our reception, and he kindly sent invitations to attend Durbar the next day. He is a fine young man, and speaks English fluently.

From Mundi we crossed another river in a flat, and encamped at Kumaund.

From there we took a short march to Dulce, encamping on the spur of the hill to enjoy some pheasant shooting.

From Dulce we ascended through a pine forest to the ridge of mountains, at the summit or pass of which we had a fine view of Kulu, and Vazeeri Rupi in particular, and by mid-day we were at Bajara rest-house.

THE END.

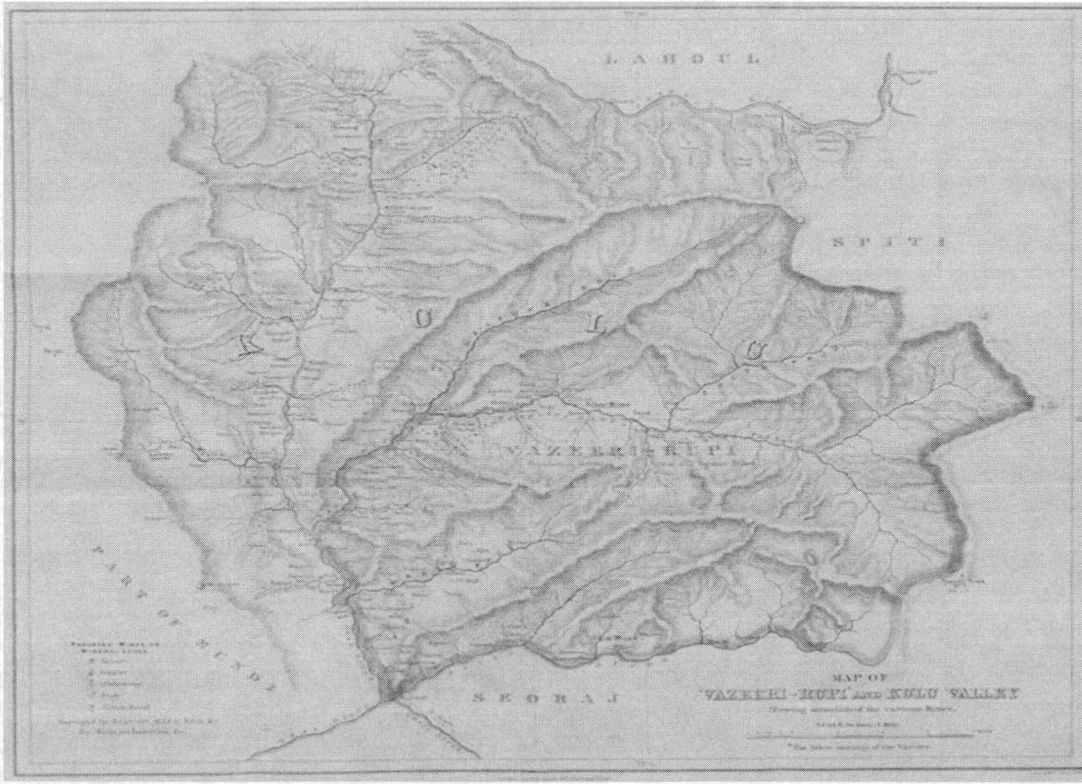

MAP OF
VAZEERI-RUPI AND KULU VALLEY
LAHOUL
SPITI
KULU
VAZEERI-RUPI
SEORAJ
PART OF MUNDI

sincerely loved and revered, either residing in this country or in any other part of the globe. As I intend to lay those circumstances before the public within a short period in the form of a pamphlet, I refrain from detailing them at present. I however trust that in consideration of the accident alluded to you will kindly excuse the apparent neglect of which I confess I am guilty, and for which I have no other apology to offer.

"I rejoice to learn that the friends of the cause of religious truth have exerted themselves in the promotion of the true system of religion in India, and have remitted about 15,000 rupees to the care of Messrs. ALEXANDER and Co. for religious purposes, and that the Rev. Mr. ADAM hopes to be enabled to resume his missionary pursuits by the latter end of this month. The time of a fair trial is approaching, and truth I doubt not will expose the corruptions and absurd notions which have gradually disfigured genuine Christianity, and have brought it to a level with heathen mythology. I am happy to inform you that the books which you kindly presented me with were deservedly placed in our Library, under the care of the Rev. Mr. ADAM. A few copies of the Improved Version will be of much use to our friends here. The Rev. Mr. Fox has intimated his intention to furnish us with a certain number of that work.

"Should you happen to see Dr. CARPENTER, you will oblige me by presenting my best respects to that gentleman. I shall soon embrace an opportunity of bringing myself in writing to his recollection.

"I have the pleasure to send you a copy of a pamphlet (a Bengalee Grammar in English) which has lately been published, and beg you will accept of it as a token of the regard and respect I entertain for you. With my fervent wishes for your health and success, I remain,

"Dear Sir,

"Yours most faithfully,

"RAMMOHUN ROY,

"CALCUTTA, *Feb. 7th*, 1827."

Such are a few of the English impressions of the Hindoo Reformer, as gathercd from the notices of him which reached us previously to his taking up his abode in our own country. We cannot close this chapter better than with the following tribute to him, when his health was proposed from the Chair at the annual anniversary of the British and Foreign Unitarian Associarion, in May,.1826 :—

"Mr. ARNOTT said, I hope to be excused for seizing this opportunity of bearing testimony to the inestimable character of the person whose health you have now drunk. His high and exalted talents are already known in Europe by his works; but it is those only who have known him personally, and who have enjoyed his conversation, that can form a true estimate of his character. It is not his talents only, although they have excited the admiration of every part of the world, but his virtues, his enlightened and benevolent heart, which raise him as much above others in philanthropy as in natural or acquired attainments." *

* "Monthly Repository," 1826, Vol. XXI., p. 309.

Chapter II.

ARRIVAL IN ENGLAND AND RESIDENCE IN LONDON.

THE arrival of the illustrious Hindoo Reformer in our country was anxiously anticipated by all who had become acquainted with him through the various channels which have been laid before the reader. The nature of his labours, and the distance of the scene of them, naturally prevented his being an object of popular enthusiasm ;—nor, if that had been excited in his favour, would he have desired the public demonstrations of admiration and respect which were recently accorded to the great Italian patriot. But the reception given to him, though of a widely different kind, must have been no less gratifying to him at the time, and to his countrymen since his departure. The highest honours were publicly accorded to him, and a place was awarded to him among the foreign ambassadors at the coronation of the sovereign ; persons the most remarkable for their social standing and literary eminence sought his society, and highly esteemed the privilege of intercourse with him;—he was received into our English homes not only as a distinguished guest, but as a friend; and when he was prostrated on the bed of sickness and of death in a foreign land, he was surrounded with the most loving attentions, tended with the most anxious solicitude, and finally laid in the grave surrounded with true mourners, who felt him akin to them in spirit, if not connected with him by the ties of earthly relationship.

At this distance of time, however, when more than forty years have passed, and swept away so large a portion of the generation then existing, it is extremely difficult to collect memorials of his eventful visit, the first of the kind which had ever been paid to our country. The answers to inquiries on the subject have constantly been that some relative or friend was in frequent and highly interesting communications with the celebrated Brahmin, and could have given abundant information,—but that he is dead! The gentlemen at whose house RAMMOHUN ROY resided in London, and who were on terms of intimate friendship with him, could have afforded the most important information respecting his pursuits there; but they have long since passed away. Those that still remain and had the privilege of knowing him were generally too young at the time to have entered sufficiently fully into his general objects, and therefore cannot throw much light on the manner in which he carried them out. From some of these, however, very interesting reminiscences have been received, narrated with an exactness which shows how deep must have been the impression which they made. From these and from such incidental notices as appeared at the period, especially from the work of the Rev. Dr. CARPENTER already alluded to, our materials must be drawn.

We do not find any record of the few years preceding the arrival of RAMMOHUN ROY in England. We have seen that he had contemplated this visit during a long period, and doubtless had been making preparation for its accomplishment. The lawsuit which he had been carrying on for some time in reference to his caste had doubtless a direct bearing on his projected voyage. We understand, that strictly speaking, the mere circumstance of leaving the country is regarded as involving loss of caste; he was probably anxious to establish that this is not necessarily the case, and succeeded;—he retained his rank, and to the very last he was habitually careful while in our country to avoid every thing that could be construed into an act exposing him to loss of caste, and he was constantly attended upon by a Brahmin, who would of course report infringement of regulations. We have already seen that his motive in this, was not any lingering attachment to the superstitions of his country, or to early associations but a desire to avoid every thing which might impair his usefulness among his countrymen, or diminish the influence of his teachings,

The immense difficulty of the enterprise at that period is proved by the fact, that we do not hear of any other Hindoo of high caste visiting this country since the death of RAM-MOHUN ROY, until, in 1841 or 1842, his friend, DWARKANATH TAGORE, came to England; and in 1845 four native Indian Medical Students accompanied hither Dr. HENRY GOODEVE, the founder of the Medical College in Calcutta. It is only at the present time, when a number of courageous young men have determined mutually to support each other in casting off the shackles of superstition and caste, and that a few have pioneered the way, rendering the undertaking practicable and comparatively easy, that such an enterprise has been regarded otherwise than with the greatest dread. It is necessary to remember this, fully to realize the courage* of the Hindoo Reformer.

The King of Delhi availed himself of the

opportunity afforded by RAMMOHUN ROY's visit to England to urge certain claims on the British Government, and conferred upon him the title of Rajah, or Prince, by which he was commonly known in this country, RAMMOHUN ROY being the only Indian Prince known among us.

It was on April 8th, 1831, that Rajah RAMMOHUN ROY landed in our country, at Liverpool. He was at once invited by WILLIAM RATHBONE, Esq to take up his residence at the hospitable abode of Greenbank, which has been honoured by the presence of so many illustrious strangers who have there found a home; he preferred however to be independent, and at Radley's Hotel he was visited by many who desired at once to give him a respectful greeting. There are some who still treasure the remembrance of being among his early visitors. One of these, now a grey headed man, recollected when a young midshipman. on arriving at Calcutta going to visit the magnificent residence and grounds of the Brahmin, who was even then celebrated; it was in the Circular Road, at the eastern extremity of the town. He did not see the master of the mansion, but he picked up in the large aviary a relic in remembrance of the distinguished man, which he still treasures. The Rajah was pleased to meet on his arrival one even in comparatively humble rank, who had visited his country and his own home. Those who had watched with deep interest his religious progress eagerly welcomed him. The brief narrative of a most interesting interview with the celebrated WILLIAM ROSCOE is happily preserved in the Memoir of that eminent man by his son, HENRY ROSCOE :—

"It will be recollected," says the biographer, "that at a very early period of his life Mr. ROSCOE had collected the moral precepts of the New Testament into a small volume, to which he gave the title of 'Christian Morality, as contained in the Precepts of the New Testament, in the Language of Jesus Christ.' In the decline of life this youthful attempt was recalled to his mind by a work of a similar character proceeding from a very unlooked for quarter. This was 'The Precepts of Jesus,' collected, arranged, and published at Calcutta by a learned Brahmin, RAMMONHUN ROY, who, having become a convert to Christianity, endeavoured in this manner to recommend the religion of Christ to his countrymen. The character and history of this extraordinary man excited in the highest degree the interest and the admiration of Mr. ROSCOE. Not only had he emancipated his mind from the dark and cruel superstitions in which he had been educated, but he had cultivated his intellect to a degree which few of the natives of more favoured climes attain. For the purpose of studying the Scriptures he had rendered himself familiar with the Hebrew and the Greek, and had improved his mind by the study of various branches of knowledge. But these were his least merits. The great excellence of his character consisted in his enlarged views with regard to the welfare and improvement of his species, and in the benevolent zeal with which he promoted every project for the extension of education and of useful knowledge amongst the inhabitants of India. Of this zeal he gave a striking proof in the erection of a printing-press at Calcutta, at which his own work, 'The Precepts of Jusus,' and other volumes calculated to extend the influence of Christianity amongst the Hindoos, were printed.

"It is not surprising that with a man of this high and enlightened character Mr. ROSCOE should be desirous of communicating; and accordingly he took advantage of the opportunity of one of his friends (the late Mr. THOMAS HODGSON FLETCHER of Liverpool) proceeding to India, to transmit to RAMMOHUN ROY a small collection of his works, which he accompanied with the following letter:—

"'Although I have not the honour of being

known to you, I am no stranger to your writings, nor to the uniform and noble manner in which you have asserted the cause or true and genuine Christianity, against the sophisms and absurdities of those who would persuade us that they are the only objects of the benevolence of the great Creator and Common Father of all His offspring. It seems strange even to myself that so long a time has elapsed, in which I have been aware how nearly my opinions on religious subjects have agreed with your own, without introducing myself to your acquaintance. The fact is, that within the first twenty years of a life which is now verging on its seventy-eighth year, I had devoted myself to the task of forming, as far as possible, a complete code of moral conduct from the precepts of Jesus Christ as given in the New Testament, in his own words; in which I had made a considerble progress; and although circumstances prevented my completing it, yet the impression which the attempt made on my own mind convinced me, that true Christianity consists alone in doing the will of our Father which is in heaven, which will is not only sufficiently, but most powerfully and beautifully enforced in that sacred volume.

"'In my riper years, as the affairs of the world engaged my attention, I have been employed on most of the great subjects of human interest;

and have written and published on politics, jurisprudence, history, criticism, science, and literature, according to the measure of my abilities, and with the consciousness, in whatever department I have been engaged, of having promoted, to the best of my power, the improvement and happiness of my fellow-creatures.

"'Some of these works I would even flatter myself may, perhaps, have occurred to your notice; but at all events, that I may not suffer the little that remains to me of this life to pass away without being better known to you, and having at present a favourable opportunity of sending you a few volumes on various subjects that may give you a tolerable idea how I have been employed, I have made up a specimen of my writings, which I have to desire, you will accept as the gift of one friend to another; in order that, if they should be received in the same spirit in which they are sent, they may in fact diminish the barrier which Providence has placed between us, and introduce us to the society of each other, to be united, during our future lives, as true and faithful followers of our common Master.

"'The opportunity to which I have above alluded is that of a young friend who is about to depart from hence on a voyage to Calcutta, where it is his intention to take up his residence in a mercantile capacity, and who is desirous of an introduction to you, for the freedom of which I must trust myself to your indulgence.

* * * *

"'We have, for some time past, been flattered with hopes of seeing you in this kingdom, but I fear I am not destined to have that pleasure. At all events, it will be a great gratification to me if I should survive the attacks of the paralytic complaint, under which I have now laboured for some years, till I hear that you have received this very sincere mark of the deep respect and attachment which I have so long entertained for you, and which I hope to renew in a happier state of being.

"'I am, my dear Sir,

"'Your assured friend and fellow-christian,

"'W. R.

"'To the celebrated and learned
RAMMOHUN ROY, Calcutta.'"

"Before this letter could reach its destination Mr. ROSCOE had the unexpected gratification of hearing that the extraordinary person to whom it was addressed was already on his voyage to Europe. This intelligence was quickly followed by his arrival at Liverpool, where his character and striking appearance excited much curiosity and interest. The interview between him and Mr. ROSCOE will never be forgotten by those who witnessed it. After the usual gesture of eastern salutation, and with a mixture of oriental expression, RAMMOHUN ROY said, 'Happy and proud am I—proud and happy to behold a man whose fame has extended not only over Europe, but over every part of the world.' 'I bless God,' replied Mr. ROSCOE, 'that I have been permitted to live to see this day. Their conversation chiefly turned upon the objects which had led RAMMOHUN ROY to this country, and in the course of it he displayed an intimate acquaintance with the political and commercial state of England.

"The visit of the Rajah to Liverpool was a very short one, from his anxiety to be present at the third reading of the Reform Bill, and at the debates on the subject of India; and on his departure for London he carried with him the following letter from Mr. ROSCOE to Lord BROUGHAM :—

"'I have the great honour and very singular pleasure of introducing to your Lordship's kind notice and attention the bearer of this, the celebrated and learned RAMMOHUN ROY, who is just arrived here from Calcutta, and of whom you must already have frequently heard as the illustrious convert from Hindooism to Christianity, and the author of the selections from the New Testament of "The Precepts of Jesus"; by the publication and diffusion of which amongst the natives of the East reasonable hopes are now entertained, that in a short time, the shocking system and cruel practices of Paganism will be abolished, and the people of those populous regions be restored to the pure and simple precepts of morality and brotherly love. Amongst the many and important motives which have induced him to leave his country and connections, and visit this island, I understand he is induced to hope he may be of some assistance in promoting the cause of the natives of India in the great debate which must ere long take place here, respecting the Charter of the East India Company; but I have yet seen so little of him, from his numerous engagements here, that I must leave your Lordship to learn his intentions from himself, which you will find him very capable of explaining in his own strong and appropriate English idiom. One great reason, as I understand, for his haste to leave this for London, is to be present to witness the great measure that will be taken by your Lordship and your illustrious colleagues for promoting the long wished-for reform of his native country. On the present occasion, I will not trouble you further than to request, that, if it should not be inconsistent with your Lordship's station and convenience, you would obtain for our distinguished visitor the benefit of a seat under the gallery in the House of Commons, on the debate on the third reading of the Reform Bill; which favour I am anxious he should owe rather to your Lordship (if you have no objection to it) than to other individuals, to whom I understand, he has letters of introduction."*

The Rajah had the pleasure of social intercourse in Liverpool both with Mr. and Mrs. ROSCOE and with the friends at Greenbank and the Dingle, where he gave the impression which has often been referred to, "of a great man,—of power and grace in his frame,--and the same in his countenance and manner."

On going to London arrangements were made to gratify his wish to be present at a reading of the Reform Bill, in which he took so earnest an interest, but through driving on his arrival to the wrong Hotel he was too late. His views on the

---

* Life of WILLIAM ROSCOE, Vol. II., pp. 413—420.

[The venerable Mr. ROSCOE, then in his seventy-eighth year, did not long survive this interview, but after a short illness breathed his last on the 30th of June following.]

subject may be gathered from the following letter to WILLIAM RATHBONE, Esq., which he has kindly given permission to insert:—

"48 BEDFORD SQUARE, LONDON,

"*July* 31*st*, 1832.

"MY DEAR SIR,—I am *now* happy to find myself fully justified in congratulating you and my other friends at Liverpool on the *complete* success of the Reform Bills, notwithstanding the violent opposition and want of political principle on the part of the aristocrats. The nation can no longer be a prey of the few who used to fill their purses at the expense, nay, to the ruin of the people, for a period of upwards of fifty years. The Ministers have honestly and firmly discharged their duty, and provided the people with means of securing their rights. I hope and pray that the people, the mighty people of England, may now in like manner do theirs, cherishing public spirit and liberal principles, at the same time banishing bribery, corruption and selfish interests, from public proceedings.

"As I publicly avowed that in the event of the Reform Bill being defeated I would renounce my connection with this country, I refrained from writing to you or any other friend in Liverpool until I knew the result. Thank heaven I can now feel proud of being one of your fellow subjects, and heartily rejoice that I have had the infinite happiness of witnessing the salvation of the nation, nay of the whole world.

"Pray remember me kindly to Mr. CROPPER and Mr. BENSON, and present my best respects to Mrs. RATHBONE and love to the children; believe me,

"My dear Sir,

"Yours very sincerely,

"RAMMOHUN ROY.

"P. S,—If the German philosopher is still at Liverpool, be good enough to remember me kindly to him, and inform him that we have succeeded in the reform question without having recourse to the principles of phrenology. "R. R."

We must now refer to Dr. CARPENTER'S 'Review" for information respecting his visit to London.

"On the 8th of April, 1831, the Rajah arrived at Liverpool, accompanied by his youngest son, Rajah RAM ROY, and two native servants, one of them a Brahmin; and soon after procceded to London. He arrived among us at a period when the whole nation was in a state of intense excitement, in connexion with Parliamentary Reform; and being well versed in our national history, and intimately acquainted with our political institutions and parties, he saw at once the bearings of the great measures which, he wrote, would 'in its consequences promote the welfare of England and her dependencies, nay, of the whole world.' Among those consequences, he lived to see a most important series of changes commenced, in the connexion of this country with his own; in the preparation of which there is reason to believe, our Government employed, and duly appreciated, the advantages which all would expect might be derived from the presence of a man so eminently qualified for the object by his knowledge, judiciousness, moderation and patriotism.

"The fame of RAMMOHUN ROY had preceded him; but the official character in which he came, together with the state of public affairs, necessarily brought him forward to public notice even more than might otherwise have been expected. The native Princes of Delhi, conceiving that they had a claim upon the East India Company to a very considerable amount, commissioned RAMMOHUN ROY as their envoy to represent and urge it; and they gave him, by firman, the title of Rajah. His official relation and title were recognized by the British Government; but the East India Company have never acknowledged either, though they always treated him with great consideration as a highly-distinguished individual. He was however, presented to his Majesty by the President of the

Board of Control; and had a place assigned to him at the Coronation among the Ambassadors. He appears, indeed, to have had no reason for dissatisfaction with our Government, either in his individual or in his official capacity.

"Mr. DAVID HARE, an Englishman of Calcutta, of well-known and great respectibility, from his earnest attachment to the Rajah, had urged his brothers in Bedford Square to do every thing in their power for him; and especially to render him those services which he was sure to need in a land so different from his own, and to protect him from those evils and inconveniences to which his unsuspecting nature and ignorance of our customs might expose him. With great difficulty they at last prevailed upon him, some months after his arrival, to accept a home in their house; and when he went to France, for a few weeks, one of them accompanied him to Paris, where he was more than once at the table of LOUIS PHILIPPE."

My own opportunities," says Dr. CARPENTER, "of direct communication with this eminent person, while he remained in India, were not frequent. Each had very close engagements and many interruptions of purpose. One of his communications, at least, on which I rested much, was lost. I had no official reason for intruding upon his time; nor had I—it would have been presumptuous if I had had—any desire to attempt to direct his views, except by information as to the state of things among our religious community in Britain. It always seemed to me that his was a mind which, while looking to higher guidance, was to shape its own course; and which must be decided in its choice by the requirements of circumstances over which the residents in this country could have no control and of which, indeed, we had no certain knowledge. I was enabled, however, to keep myself in his recollection; and when he arrived in Britain, the first letter which I received from him assured me that I possessed his friendly regard and that as soon as his public duties permitted, he would visit us. I was his companion in his first attendance on Unitarian worship in London, and in the evening I conducted him to the crowded meeting of our Association, at which the father of my colleague, Rev. ROBERT ASPLAND, presided; where the enlightened Brahmin was welcomed as a fellow-labourer, and received with every mark of deep and heartfelt respect; and where he himself, though weakened by accident and indisposition, expressed, in simple but correct language—the remembrance of which and of his appearance, presses vividly on my heart as I commit the thought to writing—his humble appreciation of himself, and his desires to promote whatever appeared to him the cause of truth and duty."

A full record of this most interesting occasion is happily preserved in the "Monthly Repository" of June, 1831 (Vol v., N. S. pp. 417—420). The arrival of the "Apostle of the East" had been eagerly anticipated. After the proceedings had commenced we read :—

"Just at this period the Rajah RAMMOHUN ROY made his appearance on the platform, and was greeted with the cordial applause of the meeting,

The Rev. CHAIRMAN.—Our illustrious friend (for such I trust he will allow me to call him) will permit me to state that his presence creates among us a sensation which he perhaps will hardly understand. It does so, because in his person and example we see an instance of the power of the human mind in recovering itself from the errors of ages ; and because we conceive that we see in him, with his intelligence and character, one of the best and most disinterested judges of the claims of Unitarianism to be the original Christian doctrine.

* * * *

"Dr. BOWRING (now Sir JOHN BOWRING).—I feel it as a very signal honour to have entrusted to my care a resolution, the object of which is to welcome our illustrious oriental friend, and to communicate all we feel and hope towards him. I ought not to say all we feel and hope, for I am sure that it is impossible to give expression to those sentiments of interest and anticipation with which his advent here is associated in all our minds. I recollect some writers have indulged themselves with inquiring what they should feel if any of those time-honoured men whose names have lived through the vicissitudes of ages, should appear among them. They have endeavoured to imagine what would be their sensations if a Plato or a Socrates, a Milton or a Newton, were unexpectedly to honour them with their presence. I recollect that a poet, who has well been called divine, has drawn a beautiful picture of the feelings of those who first visited the southern hemisphere, and there saw, for the first time, that beautiful constellation, the Golden Cross. It was with feelings such as they underwent, that I was overwhelmed when I stretched out in your name the hand of welcome to the Rajah RAMMOHUN ROY. In my mind the effect of distance is very like the effect of time; and he who comes among us from a country thousands of miles off, must be looked upon with the same interest as those illustrious men who lived thousands of years ago. But in the case of our friend, his coming may be deemed an act of heroism of which the European cannot form a just estimate. When Peter the Great went forth to instruct himself in the civilization of the South,—when he left the barbarous honours of his own court to perfect himself in ship-building at Saardam, he presented himself to the public eye in a more illustrious manner than after any of his most glorious victories. But Peter had to overcome no prejudices—he had to break down no embarrassments; for he knew that he had left those who were behind him with an enthusiasm equal to his own, and he knew that he would be received by them, when he should return, with the same display of enthusiasm. Our illustrious friend, however, has made a more severe experiment: he has ventured to accomplish that which perhaps none other, connected, as he is, with the highest honours of the Brahminical race, ever attempted: he has ventured to do that which would have been regarded with incredulity ten years ago, and which hereafter will crown his name with the highest honour. He will go back to his friends in the East and tell them how interested we are in them, and how delighted we are to communicate to them through him all our desires to do everything in our power to advance their improvement and felicity. Time would fail me if I were to attempt to go over the history of our illustrious guest,—if I were to tell how eminently and constantly he has exerted himself for the removal of misery, and the promotion of happiness. If at this moment Hindoo piles are not burning for the reception of widows, it is owing to his interference, to his exhortations, to his arguments. Can we look on such benefits as these without considering him as our brother? Can he come here without hearing our enthusiastic voices telling him how we have marked his progress, and without our proffering to him, if not our note of triumph, at least our accents of gratitude? It was to us a delightful dream that we might, on some occasion, welcome him here; but though it was a hope, it was but a trembling one, of which we scarcely dared to anticipate the fruition. But its accomplishment has produced recollections so interesting, that this day will be an epoch in our history, and no one will forget the occasion when the Brahmin stood among us to receive our welcome, and the assurance of the interest we take in all he does and in all he shall do; to which I may add that our delight will be too great if we can in any way advance those great plans, the progress of which is the grand object of his exertions. Sir, I move with great pleasure, 'That the members of this Association feel a deep interest in the amelioration of the condition of the natives of British India; that we trust their welfare and improvement will never be lost sight of by the Legislature and Government of our country; that we have especial pleasure in the hope that juster notions and purer forms of religion are gradually advancing amongst them; and that our illustrious visitor from that distant region, the Rajah RAMMOHUN ROY, be hereby certified of our sympathy in his arduous and philanthropic labours, of our admiration of his character, of our delight at his presence amongst us, and of our conviction that the magnanimous and beneficent course which he has marked out for himself and hitherto consistently pursued, will entitle him to the blessings of his countrymen and of mankind, as it will assuredly receive those of future generations.'

"Dr. KIRCLAND (late President of Harvard University, United States).—In the absence of the Hon. HENRY WHEATON, who was to have seconded this motion, but is prevented by indisposition, I have great pleasure in seconding the motion. It is well known that the Rajah is an object of lively interest in America; and he is expected there with the greatest anxiety.

"The Rev. CHAIRMAN.—In proposing this resolution I beg to suggest that the assembly should rise in unanimous approbation of its object.

"The meeting accordingly rose, and carried the resolution by acclamation.

"RAMMOHUN ROY.—I am too unwell and too much exhausted to take any active part in this meeting; but I am much indebted to Dr. KIRKLAND and to Dr. BOWRING for the honour they have conferred on me by calling me their fellow-labourer, and to you for admitting me to this Society as a brother, and one of your fellow labourers. I am not sensible that I have done any thing to deserve being called a promoter of this cause; but with respect to your faith I may observe, that I too believe in the one God, and that I believe in almost all the doctrines that you do: but I do this for my own salvation and for my own peace. For the objects of your Society I must confess that I have done very little to entitle me to your gratitude or such admiration of my conduct. What have I done?—I do not know what I have done!—If I have ever rendered you any services they must be very trifling—very trifling I am sure. I laboured under many disadvantages. In the first instance, the Hindoos and the Brahmins, to whom I am related, are all hostile to the cause; and even many Christians there are more hostile to our common cause than the Hindoos and the Brahmins. I have honour for the appellation of Christian; but they always tried to threw difficulties and obstacles in the way of the principles of Unitarian Christianity. I have found some of these here; but more there. They abhor the notion of simple precepts. They always lay a stress on mystery and mystical points, which serve to delude their followers; and the consequence is, that we meet with such opposition in India that our progress is very slight; and I feel ashamed on my side that I have not made any progress that might have placed me on a footing with my fellow-labourers in this part of the globe. However, if this is the true system of Christianity, it will prevail, notwithstanding all the opposition that may be made to it. Scripture seconds your system of religion, common sense is always on your side; while power and prejudice are on the side of your opponents. There is a battle going on between reason, scripture and common sense; and wealth, power and prejudice. These three have been struggling with the other three; but I am convinced that your success, sooner or later, is certain. I feel over-exhausted, [and therefore conclude with an expression of my heartfelt thanks for the honour that from time to time you have conferred on me, and which I shall never forget to the last moment of my existence.

"The CHAIRMAN.—The Rajah will now allow me, as the representative of this assembly, to take him once more by the hand, and to repeat in your name our deep and heartfelt thanks for his presence on this occasion."

The Rev. W. J. Fox made the following beautiful allusion to the Rajah in his speech:

"And when our oriental friend shall return, if return he must, (long be it delayed!) to his native regions, may he have to report that Europe is not only as supreme as he esteems it in sciences, arts, and arms, but is beginning to aspire to a supremacy in benevolence which shall annihilate all other supremacies, and even in the end its own, by assimilating and exalting human feeling and human character in all the regions of the world. The Rajah remarked to me the other day, with somewhat of an indignant feeling, that he had been shown a painting of Jesus Christ and that the painter was false, for he had given him the pale European countenance, not remembering that Jesus Christ was an oriental. The criticism was just. Those theologians have painted falsely too who have portrayed Christianity as a cold and intellectual religion, and not given it that rich oriental colouring of fancy and of feeling with which the Scriptures glow, and by which they possess themselves not only of the mind, but the heart and soul of man. Oh, thus may our religion appear, creating the whole human race anew in the image of the Creator !"

"While in London," says Dr. CARPENTER, "he repeatedly attended the worship of the Unitarians, at their different Chapels in or near the metropolis ; and he twice attended their anniversary meetings : but it was his system to avoid so far identifying himself with any religious body, as to make himself answerable for their acts and opinions ; and he also wished to hear preachers of other denominations who had acquired a just celebrity. He appears to have most frequented the church of the Rev. Dr. KENNY (St. Olave's, Southwark), who peculiarly interested him by the Christian spirit and influence of his discourses."

Religious sympathy must have been truly refreshing to the spirit of the Hindoo Reformer, after the long persecutions he had endured in his own country ; but every thing which related to his personal gratification was always regarded by him as secondary to the welfare of his country.

It cannot be doubted, therefore, that the Rajah's time and labours while in England were specially directed to the accomplishment of the great objects to which he had consecrated his life.

"The promotion of human welfare," says Dr. C., "and especially the improvement of his own countrymen, was the habit of his life. This rested, without a doubt, on the consciousness of power to aid in the great work ; and it was influenced by a strong conviction of responsibility for the use of that power. No selfish narrow purposes influenced him ; and if he sometimes yielded too much to the kindly dispositions of his nature, and if he always pursued his course with cautious prudence, he ever manifested fortitude and unyielding firmness when any great and benevolent object required exertion, and exposed him to calumny and persecution.

"Such was the course he pursued for abolishing the horrid and too frequent practice of burning the living widow of a Brahmin with the corpse of her husband. This he laboured in various ways to accomplish ; and in this he had a great and acknowledged influence, which should make him regarded as the friend of his country, of the female sex, and of the human race.

"There is no doubt that it was greatly through his firmness, his enlightened reasonings, and his persevering efforts, that the Government of Bengal at last thought themselves enabled to interdict the immolation of widows. His arguments, and his appeals to ancient authorities held sacred by the

Brahmins, enlightened the minds of many of them ; and made the merciful interposition of Lord WM. BENTINCK and his Council, no longer regarded by them, and by persons connected with the East India Company at home, as an interference with the religion of the Hindoos. When the interested and superstitious, as their last effort, appealed against the edict of the Government of India to the King in Council, RAMMOHUN ROY was here to oppose the appeal ; and his unwearied efforts were given in aid of that result which finally annihilated the dreadful sacrifice of the living widow, and filled his heart, and hearts of numbers of his countrymen, with joy and gratitude.

To enable us to comprehend the immense difficulties which the Reformer had to contend with in effecting this great object, it will be well here to refer to his previous writings on the subject."

"The conferences," says Dr. C., "between an advocate for, and an opponent of, the practice of burning widows alive, of which a translation is subjoined to the Veds, give us an opportunity of observing, not only the tenaciousness with which the superstitious Brahmins clung to this horrid sacrifice, and the grounds on which it was defended, but also the acuteness of the Reformer's mind, and the logical adroitness with which he reasoned from common admissions ; still more, they display his views of the character and circumstances of the female sex, the diffusion of which in Hindoostan must tend to elevate them to their due rank in society.

"'The faults which you have imputed to women,' wrote the Rajah, 'are not planted in their constitution by nature; it would be, therefore, grossly criminal to condemn that sex to death merely from precaution. By ascribing to them all sorts of improper conduct, you have indeed successfully persuaded the Hindoo community to look down upon them as contemptible and mischievous creatures, whence they have been subjected to constant miseries. I have, therefore, to offer a few remarks on this head.

"'Women are in general inferior to men in bodily strength and energy; consequently the male part of the community, taking advantage of their corporeal weakness, have denied to them those excellent merits that they are entitled to by nature, and afterwards they are apt to say that women are naturally incapable of acquiring those merits. But if we give the subject consideration, we may easily ascertain whether or not your accusation against them is consistent with justice. As to their inferiority in point of understanding, when did you ever afford them a fair opportunity of exhibiting their natural capacity? How then can you accuse them of want of understanding? If, after instruction in knowledge and wisdom, a person cannot comprehend or retain what has been taught him we may consider him as deficient; but as you keep women generally void of education and acquirements, you cannot, therefore, in justice pronounce of their inferiority. On the contrary, Leelavutee, Bhanoomutee (the wife of the prince of Kurnat), and that of Kalidas, are celebrated for their thorough knowledge of all the Shastras moreover in the Vrihudarunyuk Opunished of the Ujoor Ved it is clearly stated, that Yagnuvulkyu imparted divine knowledge of the most difficult nature to his wife Muitreyee, who was able to follow and completely attain it?

"'Secondly. You charge them with want of resolution, at which I feel exceedingly surprised: for we constantly perecive, in a country where the name of death makes the male shudder, that the female, from her firmness of mind, offers to burn with the corpse of her deceased husband; and yet you accuse those women of deficiency in point of resolution."—*Transl.* pp. 251, 252,

"The Hindoo Sage then proceeds to defend the female sex (3rdly) in reference to trustworthiness, and (4thly) to the subjection of the passions, in comparison with men; and in the close of 'the discussion he gives a picture of the degradation to which the women of Hindoostan are exposed."

The description which RAMMOHUN ROY here gives of the degradation of women in India, and the extreme cruelties practised towards them, we will not copy, hoping that they are now matters of history only. Then, we learn from him,—

" 'These are facts occurring every day and not to be denied. What I lament is that, seeing the women thus dependent and exposed to every misery, you feel for them no compassion that might exempt them from being tied down and burnt to death.' " *Transl.* pp. 253, 255.

"This horrid practice he speaks of repeatedly as murder, whenever any force was employed; and all engaged in it as then guilty of murder. It is easy to see what malignant hatred such expressions were likely to excite.

"In the 'Brief Remarks regarding Modern Encroachments on the Ancient Rights of Females, according to the Hindoo Law of Inheritance', 1822, subjoined to the Translations, RAMMOHUN ROY delineates (p. 270), 'the interest and care which their ancient Legislators took in the promotion of the comfort of the female part of the community,' and shows the extreme evils that the Hindoo women incurred by the changes which afterwards took place in the law of inheritance. In the course of his statement he says (pp. 274, 275), 'It is not from religious prejudices and early impressions only that Hindoo widows burn themsalves on the piles of their deceased husbands, but also from their witnessing the distress in which widows of the same rank in life are involved, and the insults and slights to which they are daily subjected, that they become in a great measure regardless of existence after the death of their husbands; and this indifference, accompanied with the hope of future reward held out to them, leads them to the horrible act of suicide. These restraints on female inheritance encourage, in a great degree, polygamy, a freqent source of the greatest misery in native families."

"His labours for his country," continues Dr. CARPENTER, "had, however, a much wider scope. He took an intense interest in whatever contributed, or appeared to him likely to contribute, to its welfare; and his communications to our Legislature show with what closeness of observation, soundness of judgment, and comprehensiveness of views, he had considered the various circumstances which interfered with its improvement, or which, on the other hand tended to promote it. They show him to be at once the philosopher and the patriot. They are full of practical wisdom; and there is reason to believe that they were highly valued by our Government, and that they aided in the formation of the new system by which the well-being of our vast dependencies in India must be so greatly affected for good or for ill;—a system which it requires little acquaintance with the causes of the welfare of nations to perceive, must, after the transition is fully made, essentially promote all the sources of prosperity to that immense population whom our nation is bound by every consideration of justice, as well as of philanthropy and wise policy, to raise and enlighten. Long, however, before the means were presented to him of thus publicly aiding in the political amelioration of his country, he was promoting by example and co-operation, and by the decided expression of his conviction, that means of improvement which is essential to the permanent efficacy of all others, and from which the greatest benefits may be expected in relation to social welfare, and to the reception of the Gospel—the judicious education of the young. He saw that the communication of the knowledge contained in our language, and the training to our modes of thought and reasoning, was the only sure and general way 'of improving the understandings of his countrymen, and of ultimately ameliorating their hearts'; and with the assistance of two or three friends, he himself supported a school for this purpose from about the year 1822, in which sixty Hindoo children receive instruction."

The spirit and object of the Rajah's work while in London, are thus eloquently delineated by the Rev. W. J. FOX in his discourse on the death of the Hindoo Reformer :—

"The benefits which, besides that great testimony which it was the business of his life to bear, he achieved or contemplated, for his native country, have this beautiful quality of all pure and good ends realized by pure and good means, that however local and temporary the immediate advantages, they expand themselves into the universal and enduring, and a blessing on any spot of earth tends to become a benediction on the great globe itself. The Hindoo patriot and reformer was, by the purity with which he sustained those characters, a benefactor to mankind. The good which he attempted for his countrymen is reflected and re-acts upon us. In leading them back, as he endeavoured by numerous publications, through the superstitions and corruptions of ages, to the primeval simplicity of their religion, does he not show us, and may we not profit by the lesson, that a pure theism, the original religion of mankind, is the true basis of all religion? In endeavouring to improve the manners and condition, the laws and institutions of that numerous people, was he not working good for us, who have injured ourselves, in so far as we have despised them, or been accessory to their oppression and debasement? The tyrant and the corruptor must themselves feed at last on the fruits of corruption and tyranny; while upon those who enlighten and emancipate, their own blessing returns in light and freedom.

"In the establishment of native schools, for providing the advantages of English education, which he supported at considerable expense,—in his connexion with the Indian Press,—and his able and honourable exertions to prolong its existence, by obtaining for it some degree of freedom, he was co-operating with those who in this or any country strive after the enlightenment of the human mind as the most efficient means of advancing to the possession of political freedom and of social happiness.

"In his work on the right of Hindoos to dispose of their ancestral property, and in other legal arguments, he struggled against decisions in the courts of Bengal, which he regarded as a departure from the best and highest Hindoo authorities; and which, as they tended to establish in that country the European principle or custom of primogeniture, could not but be offensive to his acute mind which so distinctly saw, and his benevolent heart which so strongly deprecated, its pernicious operation. Property, like superstition, may perpetuate a distinction of caste. This is one of the evils which make the worship of mammon not less degrading and pernicious to society than other idolatries.

"The noble exertions of RAMMOHUN ROY to stop the prevalent atrocity of sacrificing widows on the funeral pile, no doubt contributed to the abolition of that practice. His struggle with the interests of the Brahmins and the prejudices of society would not have been so long, had the British authorities, more decidedly and promptly espoused the claims of humanity. In one of his tracts on this subject, there is a noble and eloquent passage, in which from reprobating the particular instance of oppression of the female sex, he rises to the advocacy of such amelioration of their education and condition as would give the amplest scope and highest direction to their influence on the mind, the morals, and the happiness of the whole human race. And thus, also, his desire to visit Europe and America, had its source in that pure patriotism which not merely agrees with, but is philanthrophy. He had long wished to observe society under the influence of liberal institutions. He wished the sea to become the same broad highway for his countrymen that it is for the merchants, the travellers, and the literati of free and civilized nations. He wished, in the spirit of that Gospel which destroyed the partition wall betwixt Jew and Gentile, to break the barriers which divide the Eastern and the Western world. He had other and more immediate purposes. It was his hope that he might benefit his countrymen by his presence, and, if opportunity favoured, his interference, during the discussions which were about to take place on the renewal of the East India Company's Charter. An appeal had also been made to the King in Council, by the idolatrous Brahmins and their partizans, against the decree of the local authorities for the abolition of Suttees. And the Emperor of Delhi had constituted him his representative, with the title of Rajah, for the purpose of procuring reparation of certain encroachments on his rights by the East India Company. These purposes are all happily accomplished. His evidence on Indian affairs, which no doubt had its weight with the legislature, is before the public. He was present when the Privy Council gave its final, decision against the Brahminical application for the renewal of the Suttee atrocities ; and his negotiations on behalf of the Emperor of Delhi were conducted to a satisfactory and honourable termination. During his residence here he was the deeply-interested spectator of the most important struggle for popular right which has taken place in this country. And, in social intercourse, he endeared himself to natives of many countries, and to persons of all parties, ranks, and ages ; attracting a regard which no celebrity could have conciliated, but which flowed spontaneously towards that goodness which was in him the soul of greatness."

His visit to England was at a period peculiarly important. In 1831, 1832, a Committee of the House of Commons was sitting on the affairs of India, and in 1833 a Bill on that subject was introduced into Parliament. Hence his time and thoughts were continually occupied with the proceedings of the Government, and affording information and advice whenever they were required. Every thing else was made subservient to this great object. Frequently was the noble form of the illustrious stranger seen within the precincts of our Houses of Parliament, as those still remember who were there thirty-five years ago.

In the Appendix to the Report of the Committee of the House of Commons on Indian affairs in 1831, 1832, are papers by RAMMOHUN ROY, communicated by the Board of Control. These papers occupy seventeen folio pages full of interesting and important observations. The queries are searching and comprehensive, and respect the position of the Government relating to the farmer and land cultivators,—the judicial system,—and the policy of the Government in reference to the promotion of natives. The opinions of such a man, who could regard the question at the same time with the patriotic feeling of a native of India, with the philosophic and enlarged mind of a sage and a religious man, and with a full knowledge and appreciation of the views and objects of the British Government, must deserve to be fully known and considered. We cannot here do more, however, than mention where this evidence is to be found, and give a few extracts from it :—

"In the Appendix to the Report from the Select Committee of the House of Commons on the affairs of the East India Company, published in 1831, Vol. V., pp. 716, 741, several papers are contained which were written by RAMMOHUN ROY.

"1. Revenue System of India,—pp. 716, 723. Copy of communication between RAMMOHUN ROY and the Board of Control relative to the Revenue and Judicial System of India.—54 questions proposed to RAMMOHUN ROY, and his answers, dated 19th August, 1831. Subjects: Revenue System of India, Tenure of Land, Rate of Rent, Title to Land, Improvement of the State of the Cultivators and Inhabitants at large."

"2. Pages 723, 726, Appendix A. Paper on the Revenue System of India, by RAMMOHUN ROY, dated London, August 19th, 1831.

"RAMMOHUN ROY concludes this paper (p.726) 'with beseeching any and every authority to devise some mode of alleviating the present miseries of the agricultural peasantry of India, and thus discharge their duty to their fellow-creatures and fellow-subjects.'"

"3. Questions and Answers on the Judicial System of India, pp. 726 739.—78 questions and answers, dated Sept. 19th, 1831.

"In pp. 729, 730, is the following answer of RAMMOHUN ROY to question 30,—'Can you suggest any mode of removing the several defects you have pointed out in the judicial system?"

"Answer of RAMMHOUN ROY.—'As European Jndges in India are not generally expected to discharge Judicial duties satisfactorily, independent of native assistance, from not possessing a thorough knowledge of the languages, manners, customs, habits, and practices of the people, and as the natives who possess this knowledge have long been accustomed to subordination and indifferent treatment, and, consequently, have not the power of commanding respect from others, unless joined by Europeans, the only remedy which exists is to combine the knowledge and experience of the native with the dignity and firmness of the European.

"'This principle has been virtually acted upon and reduced to practice since 1796, though in an imperfect manner, in the constitution of Courts of Circuit, in which the Mufti (native assessor) has a voice with the Judge in the decision of every cause, having a seat with him on the Bench.

"'This arrangement has tolerably well answered the purposes of government, which has not been able to devise a better system in a matter of such importance as the decision of questions of life and death during the space of 40 years, though it has been continually altering the systems in other branches.

"'It is my humble opinion, therefore, that the appointment of such native assessors should be reduced to a regular system in the Civil Courts. They should be appointed by Government for life, at the recommendation of the Sudder Dewanee Adawlat, * which should select them

* This court is now amalgamated with Her Majesty's Supreme Court of Calcutta, and is called the High Court of Judicature in Bengal.

carefully, with a view to their character and qualfications, and allow them to hold their situations during life and good behaviour, on a salary of from 300 to 400 rupees per mensem. They should be responsible to the Government as well as to the public for their decisions, in the same manner as the European judges, and correspond directly with the Judicial Secretary. A casting voice should be allowed to the European Judge in appointing the native officers, in case of difference of opinions; the native assessor, however, having the right to record his dissent. These assessors should be selected out of those natives who have been already employed for a period of not less than five years as assessors (mufti), lawyers (Zillah court maulavis), or as the head native officers in the judicial department'," †

"4. Additional queries respecting the condition of India, pp. 739—741.—13 queries and answers, dated London, Sept. 28th, 1831.

"In Vol. v., 1831, p. 741, in his answer to one of these additional queries, RAMMOHUN ROY thus describes the intelligent native Indians:—'Men of aspiring character, and members of such

† The nativs judicial officers are generally versed in Persian, and, therefore, the proceedings hitherto generally held in that language would be familiar to them.

ancient families as are very much reduced by the present system, consider it derogatory to accept of the trifling public situations which natives are allowed to hold under the British Government, and are decidedly disaffected to it. Many of those, however, who engage prosperously in commerce, and of those who are secured in the peaceful possession of their estates by the permanent settlement, and such as have sufficient intelligence to foresee the probability of future improvement which presents itself under the British rule, are not only reconciled to it, but really view it as a blessing to the country.

" 'But I have no hesitation in stating, with reference to the general feeling of the more intelligent part of the native community, that the only course of policy which can ensure their attachment to any form of government would be that of making them eligible to gradual promotion, according to their respective abilites and merits, to situations of trust and respectability in the State.'—RAMMOHUN ROY, London, Sept. 28, 1831."

"In Vol. VIII., 1831-2, in the General Appendix to the Report from the Select Committee of the House of Commons on the affairs of the East India Company, Section v, pp. 341—343.—

Remarks by RAMMOHUN ROY are given on the settlement of Europeans in India, dated 14th July 1832.

"In p. 348, the following extract is given in this Appendix from a speech by RAMMOHUN ROY, who is described as an illustrious native, 'On the advantages of intercourse between the natives of India and European gentlemen':– 'From personal experience I am impressed with this conviction, that the greater our intercourse with European gentlemen, the greater will be our improvement in literary, social, and political affairs; a fact which can easily be proved by comparing the condition of those of my countrymen who have enjoyed this advantage, with that of those who have unfortunately not had that opportunity.' The speech had been delivered at a public meeting of the native inhabitants of Calcutta";

"The evidence of RAMMOHUN ROY, in 1831, is referred to in the Appendix to the Report of 1833, p. 366, respecting the condition of the ryots, in India."

"A side note for reference, p. 366, opposite to this mention of RAMMOHUN ROY, has these words, 'Evidence before Committee of 1831. Evidence before this Committee, A to G, 35.p. 5, min.,' which seems to show that the Rajah had been examined before a Committee of the House of Commons."

The literary labours of the Rajah were continued even in the midst of his political action, and the objects of interest in our great metropolis which are usually so engrossing to a stranger. We find these announcements in the "Christian Reformer" for February, 1832, Vol. XVIII., p. 95 :—

"The following publications are announced from the pen of Rajah RAMMOHUN ROY: 'An Essay on the Rights of Hindoos over Ancestral Property, according to the Law of Bengal, with an Appendix, containing Letters on the Hindoo Law of Inheritance'; and 'Remarks on East India Affairs; comprising the Evidence to the Committee of the House of Commons on the Judicial and Revenue Systems of India, with a Dissertation on its Ancient Boundaries; also Suggestions for the Future Government of the Country, illustrated by a Map, and further enriched with Notes."

In June of the same year, p. 287, we find :—

"The Rajah RAMMOHUN ROY has published his evidence before the Select Committee of the House of Commons appointed with a view to the question of the renewal of the East India Company's Charter, in an 8vo. volume entitled 'Exposition of the Practical Operation of the Judicial and Revenue Systems of India.' There is little interesting to the general reader in this work, though it will, we doubt not, have some weight with the legislature in the forthcoming discussion of the Company's Charter. We are pleased to find the following announcement at the close of some 'Preliminary Remarks:' the Rajah had just stated that he sailed from Calcutta, Nov. 19, 1830, and arrived in England, April 8, 1831—'The particulars of my voyage and travels will be found in a journal which I intend to publish, together with whatever has appeared to me most worthy of remark and record in regard to the intelligence, riches and power, manners, customs, and especially the female virtue and excellence existing in this country'."

In the "Monthly Repository" for September, of the same year (N. S., Vol. VI, p. 609), occurs a review of the two following works:—

"1. Exposition of the Practical Operation of of the Judicial and Revenue Systms of India. By Rajah RAMMOHUN ROY. London: Smith, Elder and Co., 1832.

"2. Translation of several principal books, passages and texts of the Veds, and of some controversial works on Brahminical Theology. By the same. London: Parbury, Allen and Co., 1832."

It is to be regretted that works which must

have contained information so valuable and views so important should be at present but little known. We may hope that they will not be allowed to remain much longer in obscurity, but will be collected and republished.

Having thus considered the Rajah RAMMOHUN ROY during his residence in London in his religious, political and literary aspect, we may now observe him in his social relations.

We frequently remark in great reformers, and those who have been obliged, in the execution of important work for their fellow creatures, to tax their energies to the utmost, a deficiency in the more delicate and graceful parts of the character. The contrary was the case in the Hindoo patriot and reformer. The extraordinary courteousness and suavity of his general demeanour, and his habitual care to avoid giving unnecessary pain, would have made those who enjoyed his society think of him only as a most delightful and intellectual companion, did not some observation incidentally reveal what were the ever present subjects of his thoughts. To this those can testify who have the privilege of recollecting him personally.

How much the Hindoo Reformer attracted the attention of society, and won the respect of the intellectual portion of it, is shown by the following extracts from Miss LUCY AIKIN'S letters to Dr. CHANNING (Memoirs, Miscellanies and Letters, of the late LUCY AIKIN. London: Longman). The first is from a letter to Dr. CHANNING, date Hampstead, June 28, 1831 :—

"In the intervals of politics we talk of the Christian Brahmin, RAMMOHUN ROY. All accounts agree in representing him as a person of extraordinary merit. With very great intelligence and ability, he unites a modesty and simplicity which win all hearts. He has a very great command of the language, and seems perfectly well versed in the political state of Europe, and an ardent well-wisher to the cause of freedom and improvement everywhere. To his faith he has been more than a martyr. On his conversion to Christianity his mother cursed him, and his wife (or wives) and children all forsook him. He had grievous oppressions to endure from the Church party on turning Unitarian. This was at Calcutta; here it is determined to court him. Two bishops have noticed him, and the East India Company show him all civilities. But his heart is with his brethren in opinion, with whom chiefly he spends his time. I hear of him this remarkable saying,—that the three countries in Europe which appear even less prepared than Asia for a liberal system of religon, are Spain, Portugal and England."

The next is dated Hampstead, Sept. 6th, 1831 :—

"Just now my feelings are more cosmopolite than usual; I take a personal concern in a *third* quarter of the globe, since I have seen the excellent RAMMOHUN ROY. I rejoice in the hope that you will see him some time, as he speaks of visiting your country, and to know you would be one of his first objects. He is indeed a glorious being,—a true sage, as it appears, with the genuine humility of the character, and with the genuine sensibility, a more engaging tenderness of heart than any *class* of character can justly claim. He came to my house, at the suggestion of Dr. BOOTT, who accompanied him partly for the purpose of meeting Mrs. JOANNA BAILLIE, and discussing with her the Arian tenets of her book. He mentions the Sanscrit as the mother language of the Greek, and said the expressions of the New Testament most perplexing to an European, were familiar to an Oriental acquainted with this language and its derivations, and that to such a person the texts which are thought to support the doctrine for the prëexistence, bear quite another sense. She was a little alarmed at the erudition of her antagonist, and slipped out at last by telling him that his interpretations were too subtle for an unlearned person like herself. We then got him upon subjects more interesting to me—Hindoo laws, especially those affecting women. He spoke of polygamy as a crime, said it was punishable by their law, except for certian causes, by a great fine; but the Mussulmans did not enforce the fine, and their example had corrupted Hindoos; *they* were cruel to women, the Hindoos were forbidden all cruelty. Speaking of the abolition of widow-burning by Lord W. BENTINCK, he fervently exclaimed, 'May God *load* him with blessings!' His feeling for women in general, still more than the admiration he expressed of the mental accomplishments of English ladies, won our hearts. He mentioned his own mother, and in terms which convinced us of the falsehood of the shocking tale that she burned herself for his apostacy. It is his business here to ask two boons for his countrymen—trial by jury, and freedom for British capitalists to colonise amongst them. Should he fail in obtaining these, he speaks of ending his days in America."

Miss AIKIN again refers to the Rajah, as follows, in a letter dated Oct. 15th, 1832:—

"I wonder whether you have seen a small book published by RAMMOHUN ROY containing translations of several of the Hindoo Veds? I have a good deal of interest in this view of theology and metaphysics of a nation so remote in every respect from us and our ways of thinking. The great point which the true friend of his country and his race has had in view in his various controversies with his own countrymen, has been to show that, although some idolatrous rites are sanctioned by their sacred books, yet it has always been the doctrine of the most authentic of these, that the highest future happiness was only attainable by a pure and austere life, and the worship of the invisible universal Spirit—that idolatry was for the gross and ignorant, rites and observances for them only. Thus he shows that eternal felicity—that is, absorption into the supreme spirit, is promised to women who after the death of their husbands lead devout and holy lives! and only a poor lease of thirty-five millions of years of happiness with their husbands to such as burn with them, after the expiration of which their souls are to transmigrate into different animals. This you will say is mighty puerile, but it is at least meeting his antagonists on their own ground. Afterwards he details the many cruelties and oppressions to which females in his country are subjected by the injustice and barbarity of the stronger sex, and pleads for pity towards them with such powerful, heartfelt eloquence as no woman, I think, can peruse without tears and fervent invocations of blessings on his head. The Rajah is now at Paris, where I doubt if he will find much gratification, as he is not well versed in the

French language; he will return to us, however, soon after the meeting of parliament. I dread the effects of another English winter on his constitution; and yet it almost seems as if a life like his must be under the peculiar guardianship of Providence."

The Rajah alludes to his visit to France in the following interesting letters, addressed to Mrs. WOODFORD, of Brighton, and her late husband, which have been kindly furnished by her:—

"JANUARY, 31st, 1833.

"MY DEAR SIR,—I had on the 27th the pleasure of receiving your obliging communication, and beg to offer you and Mrs. W. my best thanks for this mark of attention towards me. I rejoice to observe that the translation of the Veds, &c., which I presented to Mrs. W. before my departure for the continent of Europe, has proved interesting to her and to yourself. I am now confirmed in the opinion, that her good sense and her *rational* devotion to religion will not induce her to reject any reasonable sentiments, on the ground that they are not found in this book, or in that volume.

"I was detained in France too late to proceed to Italy last year; besides, without a knowledge of French, I found myself totally unable to carry on communication with foreigners, with any degree of facility. Hence I thought I would not avail myself of my travels through Italy and Austria to my own satisfaction. I have been studying French with a French gentleman who accompanied me to London, and now is living with me.

"I shall be most happy to receive your nephew Mr. KINGLAKE, as I doubt not his company and conversation as your relative, and a firm friend of liberal principles, will be a source of delight to me. I thank you for the mention you made of Sir HENRY STRACHEY. His talents, acquirements and manners, have rendered his name valuable to those who know him and can appreciate his merits. To the best of my belief and recollection, I declare that I do not know a native of Persia or India who could repeat Persian with greater accuracy than this British-born gentleman.

"RAMMOHUN ROY."

"48 BEDFORD SQUARE,
April 27th, 1832.

"MY DEAR MADAM,—I now have the pleasure of begging your acceptance of the accompanying copy of my remarks on India, and of another copy of a pamphlet on the abolition of the practice of burning Hindoo widows alive. You will, I am sure, be highly gratified to learn that the present Governor-General of India has sufficient moral courage to afford them protection against their selfish relations, who cruelly used to take advantage of their tender feelings in the name and under the cloak of religion. It must have afforded Mr. WOODFORD and yourself much gratificaiion to learn, by the first conveyance, the division on the second reading of the Reform Bill. The struggles are not merely between the reformers and anti-reformers, but between liberty and tyranny throughout the world; between justice and injustice, and between right and wrong. But from a reflection on the past events of history, we clearly perceive that liberal principles in politics and religion have been long gradually, but steadily, gaining ground, notwithstanding the opposition and obstinacy of despots and bigots. I am still unable to determine the period of my departure from London, and my visits to you in the country. I may perhaps do myself that pleasure.

"RAMMOHUN ROY,"

"48 BEDFORD SQUARE,

August 22nd, 1833.

"MY. DEAR SIR,—I was glad to hear from Mr. CAREY some time ago, that you and Mrs. W. were in good health when he saw you last;

and Sir HENRY STRACHEY,' whom I had the pleasure of seeing about three weeks ago, has confirmed the same information. He is indeed an extraordinary man, and I feel delighted whenever I have an apportunity of conversing with that philosopher. I have been rather poorly for some days past; I am now getting better, and entertain a hope of proceeding to the country in a few days, when I will endeavour to pay you a visit in Taunton. The reformed Parliament has disappointed the people of England; the ministers may perhaps redeem their pledge during next session. The failure of several mercantile houses in Calcutta has produced much distrust, both in India and England. The news from Portugal is highly gratifying, though another struggle is still expected. I hope you will oblige me by presenting to Mrs. W., with my best respects, the accompanying copy of a translation, giving an account of the system of religion which prevailed in Central India, at the time of the invasion of that country by Alexander the Great.

RAMMOHUN ROY."

Many interesting anecdotes might have been collected soon after the Rajah's death, illustrating his character in social intercourse, but at this distance of time only a few can be gleaned. The first is from the pen of Mr. Recorder HILL:—

"I only met the Rajah RAMMOHUN ROY, once in my life. It was at a dinner party given by Dr. ARNOTT. One of the guests was ROBERT OWEN, who evinced a strong desire to bring over the Rajah to his socialistic opinions. He persevered with great earnestness ; but the Rajah who seemed well acquainted with the subject, and who spoke our language in marvellous perfection, answered his arguments with consummate skill, until ROBERT somewhat lost his temper, a very rare occurrence which I never witnessed before. The defeat of the kind-hearted philanthropist was accomplished with great suavity on the part of his opponent."

The next is from an estimable lady who had the privilege of his acquaintance, and who was herself called from this world but a few weeks after she had penned the following note :—

"Few things could give me more pleasure than to assist you (in my humble way) in doing honour to our venerated friend Rajah RAMMOHUN ROY, but I am so miserably enfeebled by illness as to be incapable of looking over books and papers in research. I can, however, trust my memory for a little anecdote, to which yours will readily supply his courteous graceful manner.

"At a small evening party at my house in Grenville Street, principally to meet the Rajah, he referred to the doctrine of original sin, in a way that startled a lady of the low church, a very charming and amiable woman, who had brought her daughter. 'But surely, sir', she exclaimed, 'you do believe in original sin?' He looked at her, and she blushed deeply. After a minute, he seemed to comprehend the whole, and very gently inclining, he said, 'I believe it is a doctrine, which, in many well-regulated minds has tended to promote humility, the first of Christian virtues; for my own part, I have never been able to see the evidence of it.'

"The next morning my sweet friend called to apologise for what she had said, and added that she had never seen or heard any thing so beautiful as this in society,"

During this residence in London, the Rajah placed his son under the care of the late Rev. D. DAVISON, M.A., and frequently communicated with that gentleman respecting the progress of the youth. He won the high esteem of the family, by his most kind and courteous manners. His kindly sympathy was manifested by his being present at the christening of an infant born at that period, and bestowing on him his own name, "Rammohun Roy." In this child he took a warm interest:—

"His visits to *me*," writes Mr. DAVISON, "were generally paid to me in my *nursery*, as he insisted on coming up, so as to visit his *namesake* at the same time, and not to interrupt me. For surely never was there a man of so much modesty and humility! I used to feel quite ashamed of the reverential manner in which he behaved to me. Had I been our Queen I could not have been approached and taken leave of with more respeet. I was greatly struck with one thing which occurred. He called, and as he could not see me nor the boy for a little while, he waited, saying 'He would like to see the child once more.' This was just before leaving town for Miss CASTLE's, where he died,"

Very shortly after the arrival of the Rajah in England, it was arranged that when he paid his visit to Bristol, he should be the guest of Miss KIDDELL and Miss CASTLE, at Stapleton Grove, an agreeable residence in the immediate vicinity. The latter of these was a young heiress,—the ward of Dr. CARPENTER,—the former her maternal aunt and also her guardian. These ladies were introduced to the Rajah by Dr. C. in London, and the following letter respecting his intended visit, excepting the first, were addressed to them. Though they may not contain anything which adds to our knowledge of the Rajah's views, yet they give so pleasing a picture of the social and domestic side of his character, and have in them so many characteristic and incidental touches, that we will present them all to the reader :—

"125 REGENT STREET, LONDON,
"*May* 10*th*, 1831

"MY DEAR SIR,—I am now sufficiently recovered to answer your letter of the 28th ultimo. It will afford me much pleasure to spend some time in your city, of which from your and other accounts I have formed a very favourable opinion. I cannot but enjoy a high gratification in passing much of my time while there, in the house of so warm a friend as yourself, for whose proffered hospitality I cannot return sufficient acknowledgments. I fear, however, that were I to take up my entire residence under your hospitable roof, it would occasion you too much inconvenience. As I may be accompanied by a European friend and some servants, I will lodge at some hotel in your immediate neighbourhood; by which I shall be enabled to frequent your house nearly as much as if I resided in it, as well as benefit myself by the company of the Rev. Dr. CARPENTER, to whom I beg you will present my respects; and be good enough to inform him that two days ago I answered his kind communication.

"I remain, with gratitude,

"Yours most obediently,

"RAMMOHUN ROY.

"J. B. ESTLIN, Esq., Bristol."

"48 BEDFORD SQUARE,

"*March* 31*st*, 1832.

"MADAM,—I had lately the pleasure of seeing the Rev. Dr. CARPENTER, and hearing from that truly venerable minister that Miss CASTLE and yourself were perfectly well, and deeply interested in the cause of reform, on the success of which the welfare of England, nay of the whole world, depends. I should have long ere this visited Bristol, and done myself the honour of paying you my long-promised visit, but I have been impatiently waiting in London to know the result of the Bill. I feel very much obliged by your kind offers of attention to my comforts while I am in that part of the country, of which I hope to be able to avail myself as soon as my

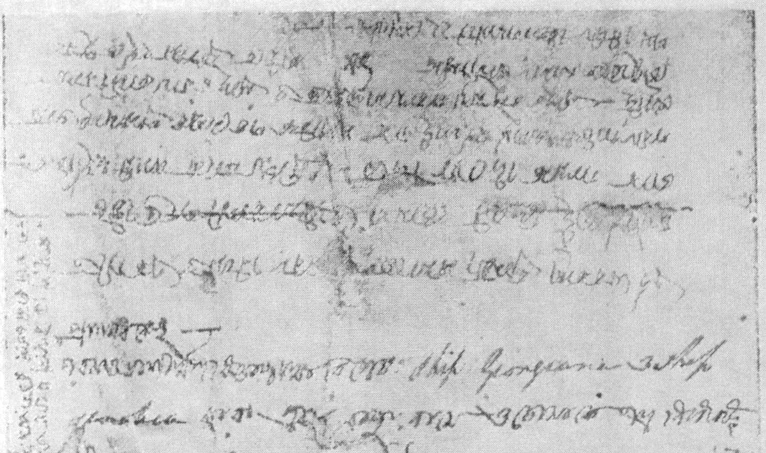

A letter from Raja Rammohun Roy to his eldest son Radhaprosad Roy, 22nd Sept., 1832.

U. RAY & SONS.

mind is relieved on this subject. You will oblige me by remembering me kindly to the Rev. gentleman, and presenting my best compliments to Miss CASTLE.

"I have the honour to be, Madam,
"Your most obedient Servant,
"RAMMOHUN ROY.

"Miss KIDDELL,
"Stapleton Grove, Bristol."

"48 BEDFORD SQUARE,
February 7th, 1833.

"DEAR MADAM,—I had last night great pleasure in receiving your letter of the 28th ultimo, and offer you and Miss CASTLE my cordial thanks for your kind remembrance of me. I beg to assure you that I am fully sensible of the kind attention you have shown me, and feel indeed grateful for it. I intended to pay you both a visit while residing in Dover, but I was informed that it was necessary to pass London on my way to Bristol. My health is, thank God, thoroughly re-established. I therefore embrace the opportunity of paying you a visit in the latter end of the month, or any rate by the beginning of next. I will endeavour to bring Mr.

RUTT with me, though I am sorry to say that in consequence of my ill health I have not yet had the pleasure of seeing him. Pray remember me kindly to Miss CAROLINE RUTT, and present my best respects to Dr. CARPENTER, who truly stands very high in my estimation. I now conclude this with my best regards for you and for Miss CASTLE, and remain, dear Madam,

"Yours most faithfully,

"RAMMOHUN ROY.

"To Miss KIDDELL,

"Stapleton Grove, near Bristol."

"BEDFORD SQUARE,

May 14*th*, 1833.

"DEAR MADAM,—During last week I more than once intended to proceed to Bristol to avail myself of your kind invitation. But *important* matters passing here daily have detained me, and may perhaps detain me longer than I expect. I however lose no time in informing you that the influenza has already lost its influence in London, a circumstance which justifies my entertaining a hope of seeing you and your friends in the metropolis within a short time, perhaps by the

25th instant. In the anticipation of the pleasure of being soon introduced to you and your friends, I remain, with my best compliments to Miss CASTLE and Miss RUTT,

"Dear Madam,

"Yours most faithfully,

"RAMMOHUN ROY,

"P.S.—I sincerely hope that you *all* have escaped the complaint. "R. R.

"Miss KIDDELL,

"Stapleton Grove, near Bristol."

TO MISS KIDDELL.

"June 12th, 1833.

"DEAR MADAM,—As Astley's Theatre commences at a-quarter past six o'clock p. m., I propose doing myself the pleasure of calling upon you at a little after half-past five to accompany you and your friends to the Theatre. In the meantime, I remain, dear Madam,

"Yours very sincerely,

"RAMMOHUN ROY.

TO MISS CASTLE.

June 22nd, 1833.

"MA CHERE DEMOISELLE,—I hope you will

excuse my boldness when I take upon myself to remind you of your promise to read the publication of a certain learned Brahmin which I have brought to your notice. You may begin with page 4, and afterwards read the preceding part. I trust our truly esteemed Miss KIDDELL is now restored to health, and remain,

"Yours very sincerely,

RAMMOHUN ROY.

This note does not request an answer.

To Miss KIDDELL.

"DEAR MADAM,—I hope you and your friends are not worse from keeping late hours. I beg your acceptance of the accompanying volume, containing a series of sermons preached by Dr. CHANNING, which I prize very highly.

"I also beg you will oblige me by rendering the small pamphlet, published by a friend, acceptable to Miss CASTLE. Being averse to induce her to write a letter of thanks for such a trifling present, I have refrained from sending it directly to Miss CASTLE. Had I not been engaged to a dinner party to-day, I would have made another trial of Miss RUTT'S generosity this afternoon. I will endeavour to pay you a short visit between the hours of ten and twelve, should you be at home.

"I remain,
"Yours very sincerely,
"RAMMOHUN ROY."

48 BEDFORD SQUARE.
July 9th, 1833.

"DEAR MADAM,—I had yesterday the pleasure of receiving your letter of the 6th, and rejoice to learn that you find my son peaceable and well-behaved. I however entreat you will not stand on ceremony with him. Be pleased to correct him whenever he deserves correction. My observation on, and confidence in, your excellent mode of educating young persons, have fully encouraged me to leave my youngster under your sole guidance. I at the same time cannot help feeling uneasy now and then, at the chance of his proving disrespectful or troublesome to you or to Miss CASTLE.

"Miss DANIEL is not going to Bristol to-day. She will probably leave us on Friday next, when I intend to send a parcel of books, &c., in her charge. I hope I shall be able to have the pleasure of visiting you at your country residence next week, and not before, a circumstance which I fear will prevent us from joining the meeting in your neighbourhood. Dr. CARPENTER (I think) left London on Saturday last. I doubt not you will take my youngster every Sunday, to hear that pious and true minister of the Gospel.

"I will write again by Friday next. In the meantime I remain, dear Madam,

"Yours very sincerely,

RAMMOHUN ROY.

"Miss KIDDELL,

"Stapleton Grove, near Bristol."

On the same sheet as the foregoing :—

"MA CHERE DEMOISELLE,—With delight I read the few lines with which you have favoured me, and offer you my warm acknowledgments for them. They indicate that I still retain a place in your memory. I hope I shall be able to receive from you next week marks of personal civility. I also hope to be able to send you a small volume on Friday next for your acceptance, with a short letter, and will earnestly expect for a few lines in reply. Pray remember me kindly to my son and to Miss RUTT, and believe me always, with the kindest regard,

"Yours most sincerely,

'RAMMOHUN ROY.

"Pray excuse haste, as dinner is getting cold.

"R. M. R.

MISS CATHERINE CASTLE:

"48 BEDFORD SQUARE,

"*July* 19*th*, 1833.

"DEAR MADAM,—I know not how to express the eager desire I feel to proceed to Bristol to experience your further marks of attention and kindness, and Miss CASTLE'S civil reception and polite conversation. But the sense of my duty to the natives of India has hitherto prevented me from fixing a day for my journey to that town, and has thus overpowered my feeling and inclination. It is generally believed that the main points respecting India will be settled by Wednesday next, and I therefore entertain a strong hope of of visiting you by Friday next. I shall not fail to write to you on Wednesday or perhaps on Tuesday next. I feel gratified at the idea that you find my youngster worthy of your company. Nevertheless I entreat you will exercise your authority over him, that he may benefit himself by your instructions. If you find him refractory pray send him back to London. If not, you may allow him to stay there till I supply his place. With my best wishes for your uninterrupted health and happiness.

"I remain, dear Madam,

"Yours very sincerely.

"RAMMOHUN ROY.

"Miss ANN KIDDELL.

"P.S.—All the active members of the East India Company having been incessantly occupied by the Charter question, I have not yet brought the subject relative to your young nephew to the notice of any of them.

"R. R."

The following letter is on the same sheet :—

"*Friday, dispatched on Saturday.*

"MA CHERE DEMOISELLE,—Many thanks for your obliging and polite communication, which, by mistake, bears no date. I am glad to observe that you are pleased with your late journey, and with your visit to Windsor. The account which Miss KIDDELL and yourself have given of my son, gratifies me very much. Miss HARE received a letter from him this morning (which she read to me), expressing his utmost joy and satisfaction with his present situation. I beg you will accept my best thanks for your kind treatment of him. Instead of thanking me for the little tract I had the pleasure to send you last week, I wish you had said only that you would pay attention to it.

"You will perceive from my letter to Miss KIDDELL that I am to be detained here a week longer at the sacrifice of my feelings. I however cannot help reflecting that to entertain a hope of enjoying the society of friends (though for a short time, say one month) is more pleasant than bringing it to a termination by the completion of it. Adieu for the present.

"I remain,

"Yours very sincerely and obliged,

"RAMMOHUN ROY.

"Miss CATHERINE CASTLE."

"48 BEDFORD SQUARE.

"*July 24th.* 1833.

"DEAR MADAM,—From my anxiety to proceed to Bristol heavy duties appeared to me light, and difficult tasks had seemed easily manageable. The consequence was that I met with disappointments from time to time, which I felt severely. To-day is the third reading of the India Bill in the House of Commons, after long vexatious debates in the Committee, impeding its progress under different pretensions. After the Bill has passed the Lower House, I will lose no time in ascertaining how it wlll stand in the Upper Branch, and will immediately leave London without waiting for the final result. I will proceed direct to Bristol next week, and on my way to [from ?] London I will endeavour to visit my acquaintances at Bath and its vicinity. I deeply regret that I should have been prevented from fulfilling my intention this week, by circumstances over which I had no control.

"I feel very much obliged by your kind suggestions contained in my son's letter. You may depend on my adhering to them. I intend to leave this place a little before ten a.m., that I may arrive there on the morning of the following day. Before I leave London I hope to be able to procure the situation for your young relative. Pray present my kindest regards to Miss CASTLE, and believe me, dear Madam,

"Yours very sincerely.

"RAMMOHUN ROY.

"Miss ANN KIDDELL."

"48 BEDFORD SQUARE,
August 16*th*, 1833.

"DEAR MADAM,—I have now the pleasure of informing you that I feel relieved, and will proceed to Stapleton Grove on Thursday next. I beg you will excuse this short letter as I am incessantly engaged in making preparations, particularly in writing letters to India and in different parts of this country. Pray give my love to my son and my kind regards to Miss CASTLE, and believe me, dear Madam,

" Yours very sincerely,

RAMMOHUN ROY.

"P. S.—Miss HARE presents her compliments to yourself and Miss CASTLE. R. R.

"Miss KIDDELL,

Stapleton Grove, near Bristol."

Alas! The happiness of the meeting in Bristol with friends so much esteemed,—the interchange of thought with congenial minds so long anticipated, was destined by the Supreme Disposer of all to be but of short duration. No visit most delightful, but too short, remained to be treasured in the memory of the noble guest with affectionate regret at its termination!—Before the letters reached India, the hand that traced them was cold in death!—And we who had rejoiced in his presence were mourning his departure!

Thou orderest all things well, O Father, and we will trust where we cannot trace!

Chapter III.

VISIT TO BRISTOL.
THE RAJAH'S DEATH, AND INTERMENT.

EARLY in the month of September, 1833, the Rajah RAMMOHUN ROY arrived at Stapleton Grove, near Bristol, accompanied by Miss HARE, the daughter of his late esteemed friend, Mr. DAVID HARE, of Calcutta, who then resided with her uncles in Bedford Square ; he was attended by his two Hindoo servants, RAMHURRY DOSS and RAMROTUN MUKERJAH. His son, RAJAH RAM ROY, was already at Stapleton Grove, as we learnt from the letters in the preceding chapter.

Stapleton Grove is an agreeable and commodious mansion, which might well be selected as an example of an English gentleman's country residence. It had belonged to Mr. MICHAEL CASTLE, a highly esteemed Bristol merchant, and one of Dr. CARPENTER'S congregation. On the death of that gentleman, and shortly after that of his wife, Mrs. CASTLE, Dr. CARPENTER undertook the charge (they had requested him to fulfil), of being one of the guardians of their only child, a young lady of great promise; they had requested him to undertake this charge as they confided unreservedly in his excellent influence, and good judgment in directing her.

As neither Dr. CARPENTER'S professional engagements, nor the nature of his own establishment, authorized his seeking the privilege he would so greatly have valued of receiving his distinguished friend in his own house, it had been arranged soon after the Rajah's arrival in England, that whenever he was able to visit Bristol he should take up his abode at Stapleton Grove, where Miss KIDDELL and Miss CASTLE esteemed it a high honour to receive him, and would do all in their power to render agreeable his stay in the neighbourhood.

After his exciting life in London, the Rajah was doubtless glad of the quiet of a country life, and we do not hear of his having made any public appearance, or sought for gaiety or places of amusement, during his too brief abode near Bristol. But almost every day, if not daily, he and Dr. CARPENTER had friendly intercourse, either at Stapleton Grove or at Dr. C.'s residence in Great George Street, and it is needless to say that increased acquaintance with the illustrious stranger tended only to increase the affection, admiration and respect, already felt for him.

In the House of Prayer where Dr. CARPENTER officiated, Lewin's Mead Chapel, the Rajah worshipped on two successive Sundays, the last he was to spend on earth in the public services of religion.

"On the first," says Dr. CARPENTER, "I addressed this congregation from words in the 18th chapter of the First Book of Kings; where, after the solemn sacrifice on Mount Carmel, and the proof from heaven that Jehovah is God alone, the Prophet of the Lord, after sending for six times in vain, received, at the seventh, the report of his servant, 'There ariseth a little cloud out of the sea like a man's hand.' In that discourse I adverted, with earnest respect, to the recent death of Mr. WILBERFORCE, who had lived to see the seal put to the accomplishment of purposes to which the greatest labours of his life had been directed; and it was my intention, when I again preached in the morning, to continue the subject, by adverting to various other facts in the divine government, where great and effectual and lasting good was begun in circumstances which called for the faith as well as the hopefulness of the servants of God; in some of which it seemed as if nothing were achieved or even effectually commenced;—

all contributing to cheer the wearied disappointed heart under difficulties and opposition, and affording abundant encouragement to 'the patience of hope and the labour of love'."*

On the next Sunday, Dr. C's colleague, Rev. R. B. ASPLAND, officiated; he says in reference to it, "I had to speak in behalf of Manchester New College. The appeal interested him, and he sent me by Mr. ESTLIN a kind message, intimating his purpose of seeing me, and sending through me a contribution to the College. He did not live to fulfil his purpose."

The work of the Hindoo Reformer had long been known in Bristol, and about eight years before, his services in the cause of philanthropy and religion were in an especial manner brought forward to this congregation, when an appeal was made to it, answered with even more than its wonted liberality, to assist in the establishment of Unitarian worship in the capital of British India.

His appearance, then, in Lewin's Mead Chapel was warmly welcomed, and is recollected by many with deep interest. He intended visiting other places of worship, as he had done in London, his spirit being truly catholic.

It will be remembered that seventeen years

* This sermon, "The Prophet's Cloud," is in the volume of Dr. CARPENTER'S printed discourses.

before, the Rajah had first worshipped with Christians in the family of EUSTACE CAREY, and received from him a copy of Watt's Hymns; little did that gentleman know how that volume would be treasured. "It was a common practice with the Rajah," says Dr. C., "as he went to public worship, to read some of Dr. WATT'S Hymns for Children; and he frequently dwelt with great and earnest interest on the verse,

> "Lord! how delightful, 'tis to see
> A whole assembly worship thee:
> At once they sing, at once they pray;
> They hear of heaven and learn the way."

Several persons well known in the literary world had the opportunity of conversing with the Rajah. The celebrated essayist, Rév. JOHN FOSTER occupied a house adjoining Stapleton Grove, which he rented from Miss CASTLE. Mention is made of his interviews with the distinguished stranger in the life and correspondence of that eminent man.

Even in cases where there had been a prejudice against the Rajah, though we cannot suppose that there could have been many of these, his personal influence soon removed it; this is remarkably shown in a letter of Mr. FOSTER'S to a friend, dated October 8, 1833:—

"I had entertained a strong prepossession

against him (the Rajah), had no wish to see him, but could not avoid it, when he was come to the house of our young landlady, Miss CASTLE. My prejudice could not hold out half-an-hour after being in his company. He was a very pleasing and interesting man; intelligent and largely informed, I need not say—but unaffected, friendly, and, in the best sense of the word polite. I passed two evenings in his company, only, however, as a unit in large parties; the latter time, however, in particular and direct conversation with him, concerning some of the doctrines of the Indian philosophers, the political, civil, and moral state of the Hindoos." *

A large party was invited to meet the Rajah at Stapleton Grove, on the 11th of September. Of this Dr. CARPENTER says.—

"In the conversation at Stapleton Grove were men fully competent to judge of intellectual power and one and all admired and were delighted by the clearness, the closeness, and the acuteness of his arguments, and the beautiful tone of his mind. In the second of the two conversations at which Mr. FOSTER was present, the Rajah continued for three

* *Vide* FOSTER's Life and Correspondenee, Vol. II., p. 94.

hours, standing the whole time, replying to all the inquiries and observations that were made by number of gentlemen who surrounded him, 'on the moral and political state and prospects of India, and on an elucidation at great length of certain dogmas of the Indian philosophers.' Admiring respect was, I may say, the sentiment of all present."

There was on that occasion much conversation on religious topics, and as those last statements of the Rajah's views possessed peculiar interest, as well as much importance, after his lamented death, Dr. CARPENTER requested a written statement respecting their recollection of them from two gentlemen who were present, Rev. JOHN FOSTER and Dr. JERRARD. These are inserted in his "Review"—

" 'To the Rev. JOHN FOSTER, Stapleton.

" 'GREAT GEORGE STREET, 12*th Oct*., 1833.

" 'DEAR SIR,—You cannot have forgotten the remarkable conversation at Stapleton Grove on the 11th ult., principally between Dr. JERRARD and the Rajah, on the subject of the extent and reasons of the Christian belief of the latter. May I solicit your opinion as to the correctness of the following position—that the Rajah's declarations at that time authorize the conviction that he believed in the divine authority of Christ, though he rested this belief on internal evidence; and that he believed in the resurrection of Christ.

" 'May I further ask, if any thing that passed elsewhere in your hearing threw any doubt into your mind whether he believed in the divine authority of Christ?

" 'If you deem the position correct, and answer the inquiry in the negative, may I, *to that extent* speak of you as among others at the conversation to which I refer?

" 'I am, &c.

" 'LANT CARPENTER.

"To this I received the following reply, which must set the question at rest. For the fulness of its statement, and for the permission to employ it, I fëel greatly obliged to Mr. FOSTER, as will also many other friends of the Rajah.

" 'STAPLETON, *Oct.* 14.

" 'DEAR SIR,—My memory is so very defective that I have no doubt your own, and that of each of the gentlemen of the party at Stapleton Grove, will have more faithfully retained many particulars of the conversation with that most interesting person, the Rajah RAMMOHUN ROY. I cannot recollect whether, in replying, with promptitude and the utmost apparent frankness, to the respectful inquiries concerning his religious opinions, he expressed in so many exact words his 'belief in the divine authority of Christ.' But it was virtually such a declaration when he avowed, as he did unequivocally, his belief in the resurrection of Christ, and in the Christian miracles generally. At the same time he said that the *internal* evidence of Christianity had been the most decisive of his conviction. And he gave his opinion, with some reasons for it, that the miracles are not the part of the Christian evidence the best adapted to the conviction of sceptics.

" 'This led one of of the gentlemen to observe, that surely the sceptics must admit, that if the miracles recorded were real facts, they must be irrefragable proof of truth of what they were wrought to attest; and that in so serious an affair the sceptics are under a solemn obligation to examine faithfully the evidence that they were actually wrought, which if they did, they would find that evidence decisive.

" 'The Rajah instantly assented to this; but I thought I perceived by his manner that he had a slight surmise that the observation might possibly be meant to bear on *himself*, with some implication of a doubt, in consequence of what he had said of the inferior efficacy of the proof from miracles, whether *he* had an *entire* conviction of the reality of those recorded miracles; for he said, very pointedly, that any argument on that subject was quite superfluous as to *him*, for that he did believe in their reality.

" 'It was of secptics generally that he spoke; but I thought it probable (from recollection of something in one of his writings), that he had especially in his mind the *Hindoo* sceptics, whose imaginations have been so familiarized with the enormous prodigies of the Brahminical Mythology, that, in spite of their rejecting them as monstrous fables, they retain an exaggeration of ideas, an incapacity of apprehending the true proportions of things, which will not allow them to see anything great and impressive in the far less prodigious wonders of the Jewish and Christian Scriptures: besides that their revolt from the belief of the fabulous miracles creates in them a tendency, unchecked by any due strength and discrimination of reason, to reject all others.

" 'In the conversation with the Rajah in a party who had the gratification of meeting him in a few days later, there was not any distinct reference to his religious opinions. It turned on the moral and political state and prospects of India; and on an elucidation, at great length, of certain dogmas of the Indian philosophers.*

* Some letters from private individuals respecting the Rajah's visit to Stapleton Grove, were received subsequently to the publication of the first edition, and will be found in the appendix.

"'If these few sentence can be of the smallest use to you, in any statement you may have to make or maintain respecting the Rajah's professions on the subject of religion, they are quite at your service for that purpose.

"'I am, &c.,

"'To the Rev. Dr. CARPENTER'. "'J. FOSTER.

"I addressed inquiries, in the same terms with first series in the note to Mr. FOSTER, to Dr. JERRARD, the able and intelligent Principal of Bristol College. Very pressing claims on his time and attention obliged him repeatedly to postpone the execution of his purpose to give me a full reply which I knew would be to the same effect with that of Mr. FOSTER; and at last he found it necessary to satisfy himself with sending me the following brief answer to my questions, which he has authorized me to employ in any way I judged proper.

"'1. The Rajah RAMMOHUN ROY expressed his belief in the divine authority of Jesus Christ, as an inspired teacher of righteousness, and an accredited messenger from God.

"'2. He explicitly declared that he believed in the miracles of Christ generally, and particularly in his resurrection, which he said was the foundation of the Christian faith, and the great fact on which he rested his own hopes of a resurrection'."

These few days at Stapleton Grove left, then, very deep traces. "Those," says Dr. CARPENTER, "whom he had long honoured with his friendship, had opportunities of unreserved communication with him, on which they now dwell with deep interest and satisfaction. Several others who could appreciate his eminent qualities had friendly intercourse with him; and arrangements were made to enable more to know him personally, who had learnt to regard him with high respect. But ten days had scarcely elapsed before the fatal disorder began its ravages; and in less than ten days more the event arrived which has filled many a heart with dismay and sorrow."

Here our records of the Rajah's visit to Bristol are brought to a mournful close.

"It was the next morning," (the 17th) says Dr. C., "that I saw him for the last time during his life. He came down late to breakfast. I perceived that he was much exhausted with excitement and fatigue of the preceding evening; and I felt anxious that he should that day have rest. His complete rest was nearer than any heart, but his own perhaps, foreboded: yet he showed no indications of loss of mental power; and in the evening of that day, he conversed for several hours with his friends of Stapleton Grove, and the intelligent mother of Mr. ESTLIN, who regards it as a great privilege to have shared in this last most interesting interview."

"I was myself kept at home by indisposition; and I was unable to go to see him till my presence was likely to prove injurious. From the morning preceding his illness, therefore, I saw him no more, till the rest of death had ended all suffering, and, as respects personal intercourse, all earthly hope: but then, with his more privileged friends who had attended him to the last, I witnessed the benignant expression, still surviving, which had so often given a charm to his noble countenance, and which those who shared his intimacy can never have effaced from their recollection."

The account of the last scenes we copy from the private journal of Mr. ESTLIN, by the kind permission of his daughter. Though it is mournful and distressing to retrace in these records the gradual decay of nature in so noble a being, yet it will be soothing to the feelings of those who sorrow for his death in a foreign land, to perceive that he had every alleviation that devoted friendship could minister, or that medical skill could afford.

"BRISTOL, MONDAY, *September 9th*, 1833.—I went to Stapleton to call on RAMMOHUN ROY. I had much interesting conversation with him; he distinctly asserted his belief in the divine mission of Christ; the internal evidence of Christianity he considers stronger than the historical evidence of the New Testament. He gave me a little pamphlet translated from the Hindostanee. I mentioned to him Professor LEE'S assertion that he (RAMMOHUN ROY) denied the divine origin of Christianity. He said he had denied the divinity of Christ, but not of his commission.

"WEDNESDAY, 11TH.—Went with Dr. CARPENTER to Stapleton to dine. Met there Drs. JERRARD and SYMONDS, Messrs. FOSTER, BRUCE, WORSLEY, ASPLAND, &c., &c. The conversation at dinner was very interesting, the Rajah giving us an account of the process, mental and spiritual, which he went through in arriving at his present religious conclusions. His belief in the resurrection of Christ, and as the foundation of his faith in the general resurrection, he firmly declared.

"THURSDAY, 12TH.—I slept here. We had much interesting conversation at breakfast. I gave RAMMOHUN ROY some account of the West Indian negroes. He was not prepared for the statements I made, his knowledge being derived from the Missionaries chiefly. Miss KIDDELL, Miss CASTLE, the Rajah, and I, came into Bristol in their carriage. They called at 47 Park Street, for the Rajah to see my bees, with which he was much pleased.

"FRIDAY, 13TH.—Saw patients at two, and at four went to Frenchay; there was a dinner party; the Rajah, Miss KIDDELL, Miss CASTLE, Dr. JERRARD, Mr. CURRY of Dublin, Mr. BRUCE, J. COATES, &c., &c. Conversation on politics. RAMMOHUN ROY attacked the Whig party for their mode of carrying the reform question.

"SATURDAY, 14TH.—I went to Stapleton Grove, and there met Dr. CARPENTER. We had pleasant conversation with the Rajah, and dined there.

"SUNDAY, 15th.—Miss KIDDELL'S carriage, with the Rajah, took MARY and me up on our way to Chapel. I gave him Dr. PRICHARD'S work (on "The Physical History of Man"), which I had borrowed of the Doctor for RAMMOHUN ROY'S perusal.

"TUESDAY, 17.—My mother went in the evening to spend a day or two at Stapleton Grove, to meet RAMMOHUN ROY.

"THURSDAY, 19th.—I rode over to Stapleton to see my mother, &c. Found the Rajah ill in fever; he saw me very willingly, and I prescribed for him. Called at Mr. BRIGHT'S counting-house to put off going to Ham Green; and at eight the Rajah's carriage came for me. I found him a little better, but still feverish. Mr. JOHN HARE and Miss HARE, with whom RAMMOHUN ROY lives, were there. I slept there.

"FRIDAY, 20th.—The Rajah no better. I came home by two in the Rajah's carriage; went out again to dinner. The Rajah had headache coming on, but it subsided on the effect of medicine. He slept in the evening, but with his eyes much open. On awaking about eleven, I found his extremities very cold and his pulse 130 and weak, with the appearance of collapse. Warm liquids and a little wine, and external warmth, relieved him, but his restlessness, changing from the bed to the sofa on the ground, was very great. I begged to-day he would allow Miss HARE to attend him constantly. He said it would be very improper. I assured him the customs in this country rendered it quite proper, and she was admitted. I had her called up after she had gone to bed, to stay up with the Rajah. He seems much gratified with my services, and glad for me to sleep here. I felt very anxious about him to-night, and told my mother I should propose PRICHARD'S seeing him to-morrow, if he were not better.

"SATURDAY, 21ST.—Miss HARE sat up with the Rajah, and informed me in the night how he went on. I saw him early; his pulse was better, and himself altogether improved; tongue no better. Miss KIDDELL proposed Dr. PRICHARD should see him, to which I cheerfully assented. Went into Bristol; saw some patients at two, and went out to Stapleton with PRICHARD to dine at five. I did not tell the Rajah of PRICHARD'S visit until he was in the house. The Rajah expressed his satisfaction, and told me after how much PRICHARD'S countenance indicated talent. Mr. HARE met us here, and highly approved of PRICHARD'S coming. I went to bed at eleven. Miss HARE sat up again.

"SUNDAY, 22ND.—The Rajah was very restless till towards morning, when he slept with his eyes much open. PRICHARD came at half-past eleven; I went in with him, but returned at three. Mr. HARE came out also. In the evening the Rajah was better, and I was in more spirits about him. He said while PRICHARD, Mr. HARE, and I were with him, that if he were to die, he had the satisfaction of knowing he had the best advice in Bristol. MARY and my mother went into meeting in Miss CASTLE'S carriage and returned. Miss HARE'S attention to the Rajah is most watchful and unwearied; she has great influence with him, making him take his medicine much better than I could. He is evidently much attached to her, and her regard for him seems quite filial.

"MONDAY, 23rd.—I rose a little before five.

The Rajah had passed a restless night, having only interrupted sleep with his eyes open. He was much oppressed all day, taking but little notice as usually, and yet perfectly collected when roused. I became more apprehensive of the event, but still am inclined to regard his recovery as probable as his death. Miss HARE spoke in the morning of more advice. I urged it also; Mr. HARE, though on his own account he did not wish it, considered it proper in the case of so well known and distinguished an individual; and principally on his suggestion Dr. CARRICK was called in. He came with PRICHARD in the evening. The head appearing the organ most affected, leeches were applied. The Rajah was rather better at night. He has expressed to me his gratitude for my attentions, looks at me with great kindness, and constantly presses my hand. I assisted him into a warm bath in the earlier part of the day; he seemed somewhat relieved at night.

"TUESDAY, 24TH.—Mr. and Miss HARE and young RAJAH RAM sat up last night. I left them at eleven; returned to the sick chamber at five a. m. The Rajah's pulse was a little better than it was last night, and altogether he was not worse. CARRICK and PRICHARD came at twelve. During the day more composed and more quiet sleep, but with his eyes open. Towards evening and the night he is always worse.

WEDNESDAY, 25TH.—The Rajah slept a good deal, and was quieter than during any preceding night; pulse 102 and weak; Mr. HARE staidup. When he reported to me, between three and four a.m., the patient's state, he expressed alarm at the frequent weakness of the pulse; extremities disposed to be very cold, but easily becoming warm when covered; he spoke very little, but is sensible when roused. I came into Bristol about twelve; went to Stapleton to dinner. The Rajah is still very poorly and weak. A mattress has been placed on the ground for him, where he now lies without changing his situation. He seldom speaks.

"THURSDAY, 26TH.—Mr. HARE sat up during most of last night; he reported to me between three and four a.m. that the Rajah's pulse had sometimes been very weak and rapid, so as to make him feel very solicitous. He was in an imperfect sleep, with the eyes open most of the night. Dr. CARRICK came at eleven, and before PRICHARD arrived we were summoned to the room by Miss HARE, and found him with an attack of spasm, with convulsive twitchings of the mouth. These went on more or less for an hour or two, and he seemed not sensible of our visit, though in the morning when I went to him, he smiled at me and squeezed my hand in an affectionate manner. We had his hair cut off, and cold water applied to the head. After the spasms subsided, he appeared to sleep, the eyes still open, pupils small; the left arm and leg appeared paralysed. We settled to have Dr. BERNARD in the evening. I staid here all day, and am getting very apprehensive about the event. In the afternoon he became much warmer, and the pulse a little stronger, but spasms came on again about half-past six. He has swallowed with too great difficulty for many hours to allow of any quantity of nourishment, and he has been but little sensible since the morning, when he gave me his last look of recognition and thankfulness. Dr. BERNARD could not come—it was useless. PRICHARD and CARRICK left the Rajah in a dying state. Nobody went to bed before twelve. Miss KIDDELL was much with the Rajah; Miss CASTLE occasionally; Miss HARE, Mr, JOHN HARE and RAJAH RAM seldom out of the room; my mother looked in now and then,

"FRIDAY, 27TH.—The Rajah became worse every few minutes, his breathing more rattling and impeded, his pulse imperceptible. He moved about his right arm constantly, and his left a little a few hours before his death. It was a beautiful moonlight night; on one side of the window, as Mr. HARE, Miss KIDDELL and I, looked out of it, was the calm rural midnight scene; on the other, this extraordinary man *dying*. I shall never forget the moment. Miss HARE, now hopeless and overcome, could not summon courage to hang over the dying Rajah, as she did while soothing or feeding him ere hope had left her, and remained sobbing in a chair near; young RAJAH was generally holding his hand. I doubt if he knew any since morn yesterday. About half-past one, to please Miss KIDDELL, as life was fast ebbing from our admired friend, and nothing but watching the last breath remained for those around, I lay down on my bed with my clothes on. At half-past two Mr HARE came into my room and told me it was all over; RAM ROTUN was holding the Rajah's chin, kneeling by him; Miss HARE young RAJAH, Miss KIDDELL, Mr. HARE, my Mother Miss CASTLE, RAM HURRY and one or two servants were there also; his last breath had been drawn at twenty-five minutes past two a. m. During his last few moments RAM ROTUN, who is a Brahmin, on Mr HARE desiring him to observe any custom usual among the Brahmins,

Death-Mask of Raja Rammohun Roy now in the possession of the Rammohun Library and Free Reading Room, Calcutta.

U. RAY & SONS.

said some prayer in Hindostanee. When the ladies had retired, we laid the body straight on the mattress, and conversed with the Hindoo servants. About half-past three or four we all left the room, some of the servants sitting up in the adjoining room. I went to bed, but not to much sleep, the event of the night being too distressing. Our breakfast party was a melancholy one. Miss HARE remained in bed. PUGH, marble mason, came out with an Italian and took a cast of the Rajah's head and face.* Mr. J. HARE and I went into Bristol, and made arrangements about the examination to-morrow. Dr. CARPENTER came out to us in the morning.† We were all of us much in the room to-day with the body, which had a beautiful majestic look. The event is a stunning one to us."

"The Rajah repeatedly acknowledged, during his illness, his sense of the kindness of all around him, and in strong language expressed the confidence he felt in his medical advisers. It was a source of gratification to the friends with whom he resided in London, to find that, distressing as

* The cast is in the possession of Miss ESTLIN, Durdham Down, Bristol.

† Dr. CARPENTER was prevented by his own illness from seeing the Rajah before his death.

the event was to the family he was visiting, he had every comfort and accommodation that a large house, a quiët and healthy situation, and attached and affluent friends could bestow.

"He conversed very little during his illness, but was observed to be often engaged in prayer. He told his son and those around him that he should not recover.

"An examination of the body took place on Saturday, whan the brain was found to be inflamed containing some fluid and covered with a kind of purulent effusion : its membrane also adhered to the skull, the result, probably of previously existing disease : the thoracic and abdominal viscera were healthy. The case appeared to be one of fever, producing great prostration of the vital powers, and accompanied by inflammation of the brain, which did not exhibit, in their usual degree, the symptoms of that affection."

"The knowledge that the Rajah," says Dr. CARPENTER, "had, in various ways, manifested solicitude to preserve his caste, with a view both to his usefulness and to the security of his property, and the belief that it might be endangered if he were buried among other dead, or with Christian rites, operated to prevent the interment of his remains in any of the usual cemeteries. Besides this, the Rajah had repeatedly expressed

We the undersigned were present at the interment of the late Rajah Rammohun Roy, on Friday the 18th day of October, 1833, in a spot under several Elms, adjoining the Lawn at Stapleton Grove, the residence of Miss Castle and of her Maternal Aunt and Guardian Miss Kiddell. The interment took place in silence and without any ceremony.

Ann Kiddell Stapleton Grove

Catherine Castle Stapleton Grove

John Hare 48 Bedford Square London

Joseph Hare. 48 Bedford Square London

Janet Hare 48 Bedford Square

Rajah Ram Roy. 48 Bedford Square London

John B. Bishop Estlin, Surgeon, Bristol.

Geo. E. Sanders. Clifton. One of the Guardians of Miss Castle

Lant Carpenter LL.D. Protestant Dissenting Minister, Bristol. One of the Guardians of Miss Castle.

Susanna Estlin Bristol.

Joseph Henry Jerrard D.C.L. Principal of the Bristol College & Fellow of Caius College Cambridge

Mary Carpenter 2 Great George St Bristol

Elizabeth Dawson Stapleton Grove

Mary Anne Estlin. 47 Park Street, Bristol.

Ramrotun Mukerjah [illegible] —

Ramhurry Dass

[illegible]

Mr Harris. Mr H Castle, Rev J Foster, Miss Foster, Mrs B Smith, & Mr Kiddell were also present but their signatures were not affixed.

the wish that, in case of his dying in England, a small piece of freehold ground might be purchased for his burying place, and a cottage be built on it for the gratuitous residence of some respectable poor person, to take charge of it. Every difficulty, however, was removed by the offer of Miss CASTLE, in which she had the warm accordance of all her intimate friends, to appropriate to the object a beautifully adapted spot, in a shrubbery near her lawn, and under some fine elms. There this revered and beloved person was interred, on the 18th of October, about two p.m. The coffin was borne on men's shoulders, without a pall, and deposited in the grave, without any ritual, and in silence. Every thing conspired to give an impressive and affecting solemnity to his obsequies. Those who followed him to the grave, and sorrowed there, were his son and his two native servants, the members of the families of Stapleton Grove and Bedford Square, the guardians of Miss CASTLE and two of her nearest relatives, Mr. ESTLIN, Mr. FOSTER, and Dr. JERRARD, together with several ladies connected with those already enumerated: and as there could be no regular entry of the interment in any official registers, those who witnessed it have signed several copies of a record drawn up for the purpose, in case such a document should be needed for any legal purposes." (*Vide Appendix.*)

The venerable mother of Mr. ESTLIN thus recorded at the time her recollections of the events following the Rajah's death :—

"Soon after the Rajah's decease, it became a subject of deep interest *how* and *where* he should be interred. Miss CASTLE, and her aunt, Miss KIDDELL, wished to have him deposited in their family vault in Brunswick Square burying ground. But this Mr. HARE, his brother, and niece declared would be quite contrary to the Rajah's positive injunction, which was *to be buried apart from all others, not in a usual place of interment, nor with Christian observances,* fearing that if this injunction were not strictly complied with, he should lose caste, and thereby deprive his sons of their inheritance, and lessen his own influence in India. In these circumstances Miss CASTLE at once offered a place in her grounds well suited to the solemn purpose, which was gratefully accepted by the Mr. HARES, and thoroughly approved by her guardians and relatives.

"STAPLETON GROVE, FRIDAY, *October 18th,* 1833.—I attended, with a select number of mourning friends (perhaps twenty), the interment of the lamented Rajah.

"The scene was truly affecting and impressive.

We all followed the coffin along the broad gravel walk, and through a winding path between the trees, which led to the beautiful spot selected, and consecrated indeed by being his resting place! Here we all stood around the open grave, in solemn silence, and watched with intense interest his sacred remains deposited in their last abode.

"We remained fixed to the spot for a considerable time, our minds filled with such thoughts as the awful scene could not but suggest, and I felt that no *words* were wanting to increase the proper feeling of our hearts. When at length an intention of retiring was manifested, a burst of grief was observed from those most nearly connected. The two Hindoo attendants who closed the funeral procession, stood leaning against the trees and sobbed aloud, as they took their last look at the grave of their late kind master. The sacred spot is in a recess surrounded by shrubs and trees, a beautiful seclusion near the lawn."

Mrs. ESTLIN described as follows the departure of the Hindoo servants :—

"OCTOBER 29TH, 1833—Mr. HARE having fixed the next day for the departure of the late Rajah's Hindoo attendants from Stapleton Grove, requested that they might be permitted to take leave of the ladies, and to express their grateful thanks. Accordingly they entered the drawing-room, bowing very low several times, returning their thanks for the many favours they had received. Miss KIDDELL then said, 'RAM ROTUN, you have, I understand, visited Mr. D. at his request.' 'Yes, I have.' 'Well, Mr. D. declares that you told him that when the Rajah was dying he prayed to 364 gods!' RAM ROTUN exclaimed, 'It is a great lie.' 'What then did you say?' said Miss KIDDELL. The Hindoo lifted his eyes and hands to heaven, and pointing in a most energetic manner upward, exclaimed, 'The Rajah prayed to Him—to that God who is here—who is there—who is all over—everywhere; to that God—the one God'!

"When they took their final leave they were extremely desirous to touch the ladies' hands. We all presented our hands in succession; to each they made a profound obeisance, bowing almost to the ground, and when they quitted the room they said, 'Oh! it is hard to go without our master.'"

The following account of the interment is derived from Mr. ESTLIN'S diary:—

"FRIDAY, 18*th*, *Oct.*, 1833. * * * The party assembled at Stapleton were young RAJAH and Miss HARE, Miss KIDDELL and Mr. JOSEPH HARE, Mr. JOHN HARE and Miss CARPENTER, Miss CASTLE and Dr. CARPENTER, my Mother and myself, HINTON CASTLE and Mrs. B. SMITH,

MARY, Miss E. DAWSON and Miss FOSTER, Dr. JERRARD, Messrs. HARRIS, FOSTER, KIDDELL and G. SANDERS, RAM ROTUN and RAM HURRY, nearly in which order we followed the body in fours; it was brought out at about half-past one, without any pall; the attendants were merely in common mourning dress, and followed the body along the centre gravel walk, turning to the left over the lawn to the shrubbery, where it was to rest. It was then let down into the brick grave. The most perfect silence was observed, save when broken by the sobs of those who attended. RAM HURRY was particularly distressed. It was a most solemn and affecting ceremony. After a long silence Dr. CARPENTER said (there were servants and bearers, &c., about) that the departure from usual customs on this occasion was in compliance with what was known to be the Rajah's desire, and Mr. JOHN HARE desired RAM ROTUN to explain to the Rajah's friends and family in India that he lay in a spot by himself, and that no religious service was performed at his interment. We saw the lid of the shell screwed down over the coffin, and returned to the house. Dr. CARPENTER read a copy of verses written for the occasion."

The following reminiscences of these affecting scenes were recently written by the present author for the Hindoo gentlemen who then visited the Rajah's grave. As they faithfully record the vivid impressions of the time, she may be excused in introducing them here.

THE RESTING PLACE

OF THE RAJAH RAMMOHUN ROY.

"We mournfully and in solemn silence laid the sacred remains of the revered Rajah in the peaceful, beautiful spot we had chosen, on the 18th of October, 1833.

"How, but a few weeks before, we had rejoiced at his long-expected visit to us! We had for many years watched his Star in the East, rising in calm solitary grandeur, the herald, we hoped, of a glorious morn to benighted India. We had seen it pass steadfastly on its heavenly way through the midst of dark clouds, and even through fierce storms of persecution, and finally rise above them. My beloved Father, the devoted minister of pure Christianity, had viewed with intense thankfulness the efforts of this noble Hindoo to present to his countrymen the 'truth as it is in Jesus' free from all the corruptions with which ages had laden it, from all the creeds and articles of man's device, that they may be led by Christ, the beloved Son, to the Heavenly Father. It would be vain to attempt to describe our emotions on finding that this

Champion of Truth had burst through all the fetters of prejudice and conventionality,—had crossed the ocean,—had come to our England,—had desired above all to embrace my Father, to whom he had long felt united in the bonds of Christianity,—had seen him,—had come to our city to be in daily intercourse with him! At the distance of thirty long years all this rises before me in its early freshness.

"My Father would have rejoiced to receive the Rajah into his own house, had he possessed fitting accommodation for so illustrious a guest. But his ward Miss CASTLE, a young lady of remarkable loveliness and maturity of mind, who resided with her aunt in a commodious mansion in beautiful grounds near Stapleton, felt highly honoured by the privilege of placing her house at his disposal. There he came; there gathered round him the wise and good who were able to obtain access to him; there JOHN FOSTER, of world wide celebrity for his unique and original writings, was a frequent domestic visitor; and there, or in his own house, my father saw him daily. How did he win the admiration and respect of all by his noble, princely bearing, and his gracious manners! How did I rejoice when it was my privilege to be in his company!

"On one Sunday only did he join with us

in worship in our Lewin's Mead Chapel. We were very happy to have him there among us. My Father had selected for his subject, 'The cloud no bigger than a man's hand,' in reference to the progress of negro emancipation, of which the devoted advocate, Mr. WILBERFORCE, had just been summoned from his labours ; and he felt the text and the tenor of his sermon equally applicable to the hopes we had for India. The occasion was deeply interesting. The melancholy privilege had been given him of following to the grave the champion of the oppressed ; little did he imagine that in a few short weeks he should be called on to offer a similar mark of respect and affection to his illustrious hearer,

"It was on the 17th of September, after the Rajah had been about ten days in Bristol, that my Father went over to breakfast with him at Stapleton Grove, and that day being my sister's birthday, she was allowed the special pleasure of accompanying him. The Rajah appeared in his usual health and spirits, and on their departure, with his accustomed courtesy, attended them to the garden gate. This was the last time they were ever so to see him. Mrs. ESTLIN, the venerable mother of our medical attendant, was staying at the house, and enjoyed his society that evening, doubtless delighting him also by going back to the last century, and telling him what she had seen at Paris, when on her wedding excursion, she and her husband were at Versailles, the last time the Court was held here, and found themselves in the midst of the great French Revolution; or how the Polish patriot, KOSCIUSKO visited Bristol, and received hospitality from them. This was his last evening of social intercourse. The next morning he was somewhat indisposed; then we heard to our grief that the Rajah was ill; then that he was worse; the best medical practitioners did all that human skill could do for him, but unavailingly; the fever gained ground rapidly, and soon the awful news arrived that he was dead! It was like a thunderclap to us! We had seen him in the full strength and prime of manhood; his noble majestic frame seemed likely to last to a ripe old age; we thought that a long career lay before him. The Heavenly Father knew best how His great work should be accomplished, and summoned this, His faithful labourer, to his rest, that others might enter into his labours.

"It were useless now to dwell on the grief and perplexity which filled all our hearts, on the darkness which seemed to brood over the future of India. Nor will I attempt to record my solemn thoughts, when I entered the death chamber, and, placed near those windows whence the living Rajah had so often looked out on our lovely English scenery, I stood by the coffin which contained his mortal remains.

"The Rajah's illness had been so sudden, and such perfect quiet and freedom from exciting topics had been enjoyed, as the only chance for recovery, that he had given no directions as to his last wishes. It was known, however, that he adhered to all Brahminical customs, which, in his opinion, did not savour of idolatry ; this was not from any value which he attached to them, so much as to avoid all unnecessary cause of offence to his countrymen, which might lessen with them the influence of his writings. Two Brahmin servants continually attended on him, and after his death they found upon him the thread indicating his caste. The attached friends whose advice and assistance he had often sought in London, gave it as their opinion that with these known feelings of his, it would not be right to inter him in an ordinary burying ground ; indeed, he had been heard to express the wish that if he died in England, a spot of ground should be purchased for him where he might lie in peace, and a cottage erected near to protect his resting place from intrusion. They thought, likewise that there must be no religious worship or rite performed at his interment.

"In accordance with these views it was considered best to select a secluded spot in the shrubbery shaded with beautiful trees, and there preparations were made for the last mournful rites. But these arrangements and necessary consultations occupied considerable time, and as much public interest had been excited by the visit of the illustrious stranger and his mournful death, my Father decided on paying the respect due to him of a funeral sermon in his Chapel, without further delay, and it was announced that on the evening of Sunday, October 6th, he would preach on the mournful subject. The Chapel-yard was thronged some time before the service commenced, and not only was every pew in the edifice densely crowded but seats in the aisles were speedily filled, and the whole vacant space was closely occupied by people standing. Never, before nor since, have I beheld such a crowd in that or in any other place of worship. All who knew my Father, or who had ever heard him preach, will imagine what feeling, what depth of spirituality, was infused into every part of the service. The grand fortieth chapter of Isaiah which he read, had to me a high significance which it had never had before, and to this day I seldom hear it or read it without thinking of the Rajah. The sermon need not be described, as it was printed. The conclusion of it was deeply impressive. Who would have thought that on the sixth anniversary of that solemn time, the voice that uttered those words would no longer be heard in that sacred place; that the farewell he then gave to his illustrious friend would be uttered to himself; that even a deeper grief would fill that House of God?

"At length all the preparations were made. The Messrs. HARE had come from London, and those only were invited to assemble at Stapleton Grove who had been personally connected with the Rajah; Miss CASTLE'S guardians and immediate connections, the Messrs. HARE and their niece, who had attended on him in this last illness like a daughter, and young RAJAH RAM, his adopted son, with the Brahmin servants; the medical attendants, including Mr. ESTLIN with his venerable mother and young daughter Dr. JERRARD, the celebrated JOHN FOSTER, my father and myself. Soon after noon was the shrine containing the mortal remains of that glorious spirit, slowly and solemnly, in the deepest silence borne down the broad gravel walk, followed by us his mourning friends, who had but lately known him in earth, but who hoped to meet him in the Father's Mansions above. The bearers wound along a shady walk, which his foot had doubtless often trodden, and there deposited their sacred burden in the appointed resting place! No voice ventured to express the deep thoughts which must have filled every breast! 'Who could have spoken over such a grave?' afterwards said JOHN FOSTER.

"On returning to the breakfast room, my Father expressed a wish to read to all present what he felt to be in harmony with the occasion, and to my surprise and confusion he read these sonnets, in which I had endeavoured to express my feelings, however inadequately. Then we separated to our homes."

The following sonnets are those composed after the death of the Rajah, and read by Dr. CARPENTER on the solemn occasion:—

SONNETS

ON THE INTERMENT

OF THE

RAJAH RAMMOHUN ROY,

AT STAPLETON GROVE,

FRIDAY, the 18th of October, 1833.

I

THY Nation sat in darkness, for night
Of pagan gloom was o'er it :—Thou wast born
Midst superstition's ignorance forlorn :
Yet in thy breast there glow'd a heavenly light
Of purest truth and love ; and to thy sight
Appear'd the day-star of approaching morn.
What ardent zeal did then thy life adorn,
From deep degrading guilt to lead aright
Thy fallen people ; to direct their view
To that bless'd Sun of Righteousness, whence beams
Guidance to all that seek it—faithful—true ;
To call them to the Saviour's living streams.
The cities of the East have heard thy voice—
"Nations behold your God ! rejoice—rejoice."

Is. xl. 9.

II.

Exil'd from home, e'en in thy earliest youth,
The healing balm of woman's love was pour'd
Into thy troubled breast: and thence were stor'd
Deep springs of gratitude and pitying ruth.—
To lead thy race to that primeval truth
Which, bright and pure, on all alike bestow'd,
Points heavenward; and to guide them on the road
Of Christian faith—was thine: but yet to soothe
Neglected woman; to assert her right
To drink of wells of everlasting life;
To snatch her, trembling midst the dismal night
Of pagan horrors, from the fiery strife
Of dark-soul'd zealots—*this* must wake our love,
This fervent raise our thanks for thee above.

III.

Far from thy native clime, a sea-girt land
Sits thron'd among the nations;—in the breasts
Of all her sons immortal Freedom rests;
And of her patriots many a holy band
Have sought to rouse the world from the command
Of that debasing Tyrant who detests
The reign of truth and love. At their behests
The slave is free; and Superstition's hand
Sinks powerless.—Hitherward thy steps were bent
To seek free commune with each kindred soul,
Whose highest powers are ever willing lent
To free their race from folly's dark control,
To our blest Isle thou didst with transport come:
Here hast thou found thy last, thy silent home.

IV.

Thy work thou didst fulfil while yet 'twas day ;
And still right-onward towards thy beacon tend
With faith and zeal. And now thy footsteps bend
Where Christian friendship offers thee the stay
Of sympathy and love. But who shall say
What joy was ours, the eager ear to lend
To all the accents, and thy steps attend ?—
The Angel of the Lord hath called away
His faithful servant, at the evening hour,
While glowing tints still gild the western sky.
Yet though around our hearts dark sorrows lour,
And tears of sad regret must dim the eye,
We mourn not without hope. Thy race is run,
Enter thy rest ! Servant of God—"Well done" !

V.

Bright hopes of immortality were given
To guide thy dubious footsteps, and to cheer
Thine earthly pilgrimage. How firm and clear
Arose thy faith, that as the Lord hath risen,
So all his followers shall meet in heaven !—
Thou art gone from us ; but thy memory, dear
To all that knew thee, fades not : still we hear
And see thee yet as with us :—ne'er are riven
The bands of Christian love !—Thy mortal frame
With us is laid in holy silent rest :
Thy spirit is immortal ; and thy name
Shall by thy countrymen be ever blest.
E'en from the tomb thy words with power shall rise,
Shall touch their hearts, and bear them to the skies.

BRISTOL, *Oct.* 1833.

Chapter IV.

TRIBUTES TO THE RAJAH'S MEMORY.

It was indeed an appalling event,—a deeply affecting dispensation of Providence, which so unexpectedly deprived India of her noble son, and the world of one of the most remarkable men which the century has produced.

The hopes of all who loved mankind, and who felt an especial interest in that great country which had become so closely connected with our own, had been raised to very high expectation by the steady unwavering progress of the great Hindoo Reformer. Having watched him at a distance with high admiration, we had the privilege of receiving him into our homes and our social circles;—we had seen him in the midst of the attractions of our capital, steadily keeping in view his great object of promoting the welfare of his country, and making the gratification of any private wishes yield to this. We had witnessed his intense interest in the general diffusion of free principles, especially in England, a country whose destiny must so materially influence the East. Those who had any acquaintance with the less public proceedings of the Government, had observed how ready and able he was to afford all needed information ;—how courteous, humble and respectful in giving it ;—how firm and persevering in adhering to the course of duty ;—how patient and assiduous in waiting for and seeking the proper opportunities.

We trusted that he was now to rest awhile in the enjoyment of the intercourses of friendship, thus preparing to return with renewed strength to carry to his countrymen new light, and the assurances of help and sympathy from their brethren in England.

But it was not so ordered. The sun of India went down with tropical suddenness, and left us in the deepest gloom. We were bewildered and cast down. The noble form of him in whom we had seen the embodiment of all that was good and noble and lovable, and which had appeared likely to last for many long years, was laid low in death, even while the thought of him in apparent health and strength was fresh in our remembrance. He passed away without one message to his countrymen,—without one last testimony to the truths which he had laboured to establish,—without one expressed wish as to the future of his family, and especially of his adopted son, left thus in the land of strangers! He believed from the commencement of his illness that the hand of death was upon him, but, though his spirit was frequently in prayer, and though while consciousness remained he could give a loving, grateful look, and an affectionate pressure of the hand to those who were tenderly caring for him, disease checked all utterance of his wishes. Thus, too, was it ordered. In that solemn hour his faith in the Eternal Spirit resigned the labours of his life to higher keeping than his own, and his confidence in his friends left all else to them without distrust or anxiety. His faith had a sure foundation,—for it was based on that revelation of the Father of our spirits which was made by his well-beloved Son.

At this distance of time we can perceive some of the reasons of that appointment which appeared at the time so mysterious. India was not at that period prepared fully to appreciate its great reformer. Had he returned to his own country he might have received even greater opposition and persecution than he had before experienced; had he died there, it is not likely that the event would have excited any special interest at the time, judging from the remarkable want of it which was there manifested at the period of his decease. But now that forty years have witnessed great changes in his native land,—that some of his views have made much progress among his countrymen,—that important alterations have taken place in the position of our Government in reference to India, tending to remove the feeling of separation between the two nations,—it is now that the fact of the sacred remains of the Rajah RAMMOHUN ROY being laid in our country forms a kind of tie of relationship between us, while the reverence and love with which we treasure the memory of our distinguished guest are a token to them of our sympathy with themselves, and may give to his writings an added claim on their attention.

The death of the Hindoo Reformer attracted much attention in the journals of the day, and drew public notice to his life and labours. In all that we have met with, however, the sources of information were the same only as have already been laid before the reader in this volume, and it would be unnecessary to repeat them. We shall present therefore in this chapter such private testimonies of respect as have been preserved to us.

The testimony of the family of the Mr. HARES, with whom the Rajah resided in London, has been given to us by Dr. CARPENTER. He says,—

"From this family I have received every advantage I could desire, in forming or confirming my opinions as to the Rajah's habits and character; and to the several members of it, his other personal friends must feel grateful for the numerous sources of comfort which he enjoyed among them. Mr. ARNOTT (in the 'Athenæum') says, with perfect justice, that they 'discharged the duties of hospitality towards him, ever since his arrival in England, with a kindness, delicacy, and entire disinterestedness, which are honourable to the English character.'

"Possessed of the Rajah's unbounded confidence, acquainted with all his movements, and enabled to judge with complete accuracy of his habits and dispositions, the unhesitating and unequivocal testimony of this family, one and all, to the unvarying purity of his conduct and the refined delicacy of his sentiments, is as decisive as it is valuable. I had, myself, repeated opportunities of observing with what earnest respect he appreciated true delicacy in the female character: and I learn that, while he always maintained his habitual politeness to the sex, and may therefore have misled the superficial observer, he manifested a very prompt and clear discrimination as to individuals; and that he commonly expressed strong dislike, and even disgust where they seemed to him to depart from that true modesty which is essential to its excellence.

"Mr. JOSEPH HARE—his brother fully agreeing with him—assures me, that the Rajah was constantly in the habit of dictating, to those who were for the time acting as amanuenses, in phraseology requiring no improvement, whether for the press or for the formation of official documents—such verbal amendments only excepted, as his own careful revision supplied before the final completion of the manuscript: that he often had recourse to friends to write from his dictation; among others to himself and the members of his family: that it is his full conviction, that, from the day of the Rajah's arrival in this country, he stood in no need of any assistance except that of a mere *mechanical* hand to write: and that he has often been struck—and recollects that he was particularly so at the time the Rajah was writing his 'Answers to the Queries on the Judicial and Revenue Departments'—with his quick and correct diction, and his immediate perception of occasional errors when he came to revise the matter. These facts I and others have repeatedly heard from the Mr. HARES; and I rest with conviction upon them. ' It is happy for the Rajah's memory that he lived in the closest intimacy and confidence with friends who, are able and willing to defend it, wherever truth and justice require."

Mrs. ESTLIN recorded at the time some interesting particulars which she learnt from Miss HARE. "The Rajah read the Scriptures daily in Hebrew and Greek. Miss HARE often read them to him also;—this was never omitted at night. He was also in a constant habit of prayer, and was not interrupted in this by her presence;—whether sitting or riding he was frequently in prayer. He told Miss H. that whenever an evil thought entered into his mind he prayed. She said, 'I do not believe you ever have an evil thought.' He answered, 'O yes, we are all liable to evil thoughts.'"

A touching mark of respect to the memory of her illustrious guest was given by Miss CASTLE.* A fine painting of the Rajah by BRIGGS, R. A., was brought to Bristol for exhibition; Miss CASTLE purchased it and presented it to the Bristol Philosophical Institution, that all who visit the place of his death may there see his living likeness. It is from this beautiful picture that the frontispiece is taken. The Rajah's personal appearance, which is well represented in this picture,

* This estimable young lady did not long survive the Rajah. After a tedious and wearing illnes she died December 3, 1835 aged 22.

is thus described in the *Asiatic Journal*, as quoted by Dr. CARPENTER in the appendix to his sermon :—

"'The person of RAMMOHUN ROY was a very fine one. He was nearly six feet high ; his limbs were robust and well-proportioned, though latterly, either through age or increase of bulk, he appeared rather unwieldy and inactive. His face was beautiful ; the features large and manly, the forehead lofty and expanded, the eyes dark and animated, the nose finely curved and of due proportion, the lips full, and the general expression of the countenance that of intelligence and benignity. The best portrait of him extant, is a full-sized one by BRIGGS. It is a good picture, as well as an admirable likeness.' This portrait is now exhibiting in the Bristol Institution. I fully concur," Dr. C. continues, "in the *Journal's* praise of it. It gives, indeed, the impression of a less bulky person than the Rajah's was, in at least the later part of life ; and the mouth does not satisfy me in its form or its expression : but the rest of the countenance, the attitude of figure, and the hands—beautifully significant, as well as masterly painted—give that expression to the whole which those who contemplate RAMMOHUN ROY as the Hindoo Sage and Reformer would most desire. It is the expression of devout, reflecting, benignant philanthropy ;

hopeful, yet with a tinge of pensive solicitude; looking onward, and upward, and contemplating the gleams of truth and righteousness breaking forth to enlighten and to bless his country."

Miss AIKIN thus writes of the Rajah to Dr. CHANNING, in a letter dated Hampstead, Oct. 23, 1833:—

"I have had your line by Dr. TUCKERMAN. I was in Kent when he called here, and therefore only saw him last week, but I am exceedingly struck and delighted with him, and impatient to hear him speak more of his noble exertions and designs. On Thursday next I hope he and Mr. PHILLIPS will meet over my breakfast table my friend Mr. LE BRETON and dear JOANNA BAILLIE. You will be with us in spirits, for many associations will bring you to the minds of all of us. When I have the privilege to be present at a meeting like this, of the gifted and the excellent from the far ends of the earth, it seems to me a foretaste of the happiness reserved for the world of spirits. Alas for one who gave me this feeling beyond all others—the admirable RAMMOHUN ROY! He has been frustrated of one of his cherished hopes, that of seeing you face to face, either in this or the other hemisphere—but you were no strangers to each other. Scarcely any description can do justice to his admirable qualities, and the charms of his society, his extended knowledge, his comprehension of mind, his universal philanthropy, his tender humanity, his genuine dignity mixed with perfect courtesy, and the most touching humility. His memory I shall cherish with affectionate reverence on many accounts, but the character in which I best love to contemplate him is that of the friend and champion of woman. It is impossible to forget his righteous zeal against polygamy, his warm approval of the freedom allowed to women in Europe, his joy and pious gratitude for the abolition of *suttee.* Considering the prejudices of birth and education with which he had to contend, his constant advocacy of the rights and interests of the weaker sex seems to me the very strongest proof of his moral and intellectual greatness."

The following letter from Dr. BOOTT, an American physician of London, to Mr. ESTLIN, is a most valuable testimony to the Rajah's religious character :—

"24, GOWER STREET, BEDFORD SQUARE,

"*November 27th*, 1833.

"MY DEAR SIR,—Your kind, most kind letter of yesterday, has this moment reached me, and I have shed tears over it, at the fresh recollection of the sorrow that has thrown a deep shadow over the future hopes and happiness of my life. I feel the most sincere gratitude to you for your valuable services, and your devotion and tenderness over the sick bed of our late beloved friend. God knows I have deeply sympathised with you in the painful responsibility of your situation, and I am well assured that everything which the soundest medical judgment, and the deepest solicitude could suggest, was done. In the feelings of all around me here, who dearly loved him, you and Dr. PRICHARD are spoken of with sincere and grateful respect, and the blessing of a just man made perfect now rests upon you.

"Your account of the change in your feelings towards the Rajah, from the influence of the reports that had reached you, has very deeply affected me; for knowing the Rajah so well, it is the most striking evidence of the force of human prejudice that I have hitherto met with,—I mean on the part of those who misrepresented him to you; for your yielding to those representations arose from the same sensibility that led you first to admire him in his works. I thank God that you had an opportunity of tearing yourself the veil from your eyes, and that the primitive love and admiration you cherished for him was confirmed by your personal intercourse with him;

confirmed to be rendered immutable by the seal of Death !

"To me he stood alone in the single majesty of, I had almost said, perfect humanity. No one in past history, or in present time, ever came before my judgment clothed in such wisdom, grace and humility. I knew of no tendency even to error. To say he was not the disciple of Christ, that he even smiled in approbation of infidelity, and joined those thoughtless and weak and ignorant men who set themselves up against the testimonies of the human heart, which asserts the truth of religion against the wit and the follies of the vainest and the cleverest head, is to belie his whole life. I have often talked with him on religious subjects and have seen him amid sceptics. He was never more free and unembarrassed and cheerful, than when arguing with those who had a logical and acute mind. He often told me that he always introduced the subject when he met the historian of India, and that his object in the argument was to show the insufficiency of human reason for the production of the highest moral worth, and the highest happiness. He even contended that 'the Spirit that was in Christ Jesus', and unknown and unrevealed till his mission, directed the human mind to more elevated, purer, and more disinterested thoughts, motives and actions, than the noblest philosophy of antiquity did or could do; that the Christian precepts left nothing to desire or to hope for through futurity; that, as a system of morality, it was alone able to lead to purity and happiness here, and to form the mind for any conceivable state of advancement hereafter. He often beautifully said, 'I can never hope in my day to find mankind of one faith, and it is my duty to exercise the charities of life with all men.' He did not go about with the spirit of proselytism. He argued only for the sense of religious obligation, and emphatically assured us that all his experience of life had exhibited to him virtue and selfrespect and happiness in its true elements, even in proportion to the intensity of that sense. He was the humblest of human beings, and ardent as he was in the faith of his selection, he was sensibly disturbed if religion was spoken highly of, or argued but reverentially before woman. He would often smile and speak jocosely when the turn of the discussion made him uneasy from his sensibilities towards woman being awakened; and those who knew him, saw by his manner and looks that he adopted this lightness of manner in hopes that the subject would be dropped.

"I was once in his presence where a father was expressing doubts of Christianity before two of his daughters, who were near forty, and before three other ladies.' He expressed himself most forcibly in defence of the immutable truth of the religion, and when the conversation was resumed by the sceptic, he touched lightly and with levity on the diction and expressions of the other, and often in the interval sat as if he were abstracted and unconcerned in what was said; and when appealed to, he in the same careless manner criticised the language of his opponent, without touching the sense. A lady whom he loved sat by me, and said in an under tone to me, 'The Rajah appears to smile at everything.' I replied, Your words import more than you mean, and you mistake his present feelings; he is visibly distressed, and wishes the subject to be dropped.' She observed him closely, and said I was right, as he took an early opportunity of calling his attention to something else. He soon after left the party. I had an engagement with him the next morning, and the first subject he spoke of was the conversation the night before, and he expressed himself highly offended that a father should, before his own daughters, confess his infidelity and so far forget himself as to say anything to shake the faith of a female. He added, 'it is more painful to me to argue with sceptics before women, for there is no hope of its leading to good, and there must be pain where it is our duty to give pleasure always; I never permitted religion to be discussed before my daughters or wife.' I can only say that at every visit my admiration of him grew with my intimacy with his mind and actions. He was the most liberal, the most amiable, and the most candid of men. His generosity was unbounded; his most touching politeness was an instinct of his nature; it never left him to his most familiar associates; while he paid just deference to rank, in obedience to the conventional etiquette of society, he honoured above all men the poor gardener whom he met with in some rich establishment in India, who had, uninfluenced by the authority of his superiors, examined the Scriptures, and adopted the faith of the Unity of God. He went to the garden every day to talk with him, and he often said to us, 'I could have taken him in my arms as a brother.' I called with him on Dr. TUCKERMAN, Mr. DEWEY, and Mr. PHILLIPS, of America, and when he had shaken hands with them he said, with his countenance lighted up with animation, 'I am so happy to be with Unitarians. He did not mix in the sect as some expected, and reflections were often passed upon him. Mr. Fox has touched this with admirable force in his sermon. The object of the Rajah was to mix with and know all sects. One of his greatest desires was to see Catholicism at Rome. He admired the obedience to duties in the Catholics, and always spoke of them in this light with admiration. Whatever faults were mixed with their faith, he recognised in their attention to the poor and sick, the noblest spirit of Christianity. One of the last arguments I heard from him was his defence of them, against one who urged their acting under an artificial stimulus. He contended that what they did was enforced on all, by the very example of Christ; and that the stimulus was their faith in the force and truth of that example.

"But I must stop. When I think that I shall see him no more; that the beauty of his countenance, the picturesqueness of his eastern costume, the kind reception, the noble example of virtues I never felt, at least so powerfully, in others, the hope I had entertained of his future usefulness, the certainty I had of his present happiness, and all his enlarged affections,—when I think that these have passed away for the forever of my brief existence, I feel a sorrow such as I never felt before, and one which can only find consolation in that pure religion of which he was so able a defender. His loss has given tenfold value in my mind to his writings, and I have studied them with a subdued feeling since his death, and risen from their perusal with a more confirmed conviction of his having been unequalled in past or present time. Peace to his sacred memory!

"Present my best respects to Miss ACLAND and Dr. CARPENTER, and believe me,

"My dear Sir,

"Sincerely and gratefully yours,

'T. BOOTT."

Dr. BOOT speaks of accompanying the Rajah to visit Dr. TUCKERMAN, the originator of Domestic Missions, whose devotion to his work exhausted his physical strength, and led him to seek restoration in our country; Dr. TUCKERMAN was an intimate friend of Dr. CHANNING, with whose spirit he had so long held valued communion. This meeting with one of the most devoted followers of the Saviour, and one who had deeply imbibed his spirit, was afterwards spoken of by the Rajah with deep interest. Its effect on Dr. TUCKERMAN himself was thus described by him in a letter to Dr. CARPENTER :—

"I had interchanged a few letters with that great and excellent man while he was in Calcutta; and had looked with the highest interest to the hour when I should see him in England. And devoutly do I thank our heavenly Father that I was permitted to see him. Before I met him here, he was, however, comparatively only an object to me of exalted admiration. But I had not been an hour with him, before that revelation was made to me of his heart, which called forth the far higher and more delightful sentiment of *love.* Yes, in the acquaintance of an hour he became to me an object of very high and strong affection; for I saw in him the most unequivocal evidence of an advancement in Christian piety and virtue,—which I have seen in few, of those very few, who have been born and reared under the strongest lights, and best influences of our religion."

The following poetical tributes to the Rajah's memory evidence the deep feeling which his character and death excited :—

THE INTERMENT OF THE RAJAH RAMMOHUN ROY, AT STAPLETON GROVE.

BY MISS DALE.

NO VOICE, no whisper broke the deep repose,
When to the earth that sacred dust was given;
All silently the sacrifice arose
From kindling hearts, in one pure flame, to Heaven.
Pure from the sun of righteousness it came
Upon those hearts. Language, to common thought

Tomb of Raja Rammohun Roy, at Arnos Vale Cemetry.

U. RAY & SONS.

Interpreter, had dimmed that holy flame
Or, with the prism's power, to sight had brought
The varying hues which human frailty throws
O'er things divine. Oh! never more misplaced,
Than at that grave where narrow bounds inclose
Him, whose diffusive love had all mankind embraced.

STAPLETON GROVE.

THE RAJAH'S TOMB.

BY MISS ACLAND.

THIS is the spot! There needs no sculptured line;
No column marks the Rajah's lonely tomb;
But shadowing elms their drooping boughs incline,
And shroud his cold remains in sacred gloom.

Yes; far from Ganges' consecrated wave,
Beneath our pallid groves, and northern skies,
A stranger's hand hath laid thee in thy grave,
And strangers' tears have wept thine obsequies.

A stranger? No; thy "caste" was human kind;
Thy home—wherever Freedom's beacon shone;
And England's noblest hearts exalting shrined
The turband offspring of a burning zone.

Pure generous mind! all that was just and true,—
All that was lovely, holiest, brightest, best—
Kindled thy soul of eloquence anew,
And woke responsive chords in every breast.

Sons of the western main around thee hung,
While Indian lips unfolded Freedom's laws,
And grateful woman heard the Brahmin's tongue
Proclaim her worth, and plead her widowed cause.

Ah ! why did Fortune dash, with bitter doom,
  That cup of high communion from thine hand,
And scatter, darkly withering o'er the tomb,
  The blessings gathered for thy native land ?

Be hushed our murmurs ! He whose voice had won
  Thee. heav'n bound trav'ler, forth from Pagan night,
In mercy called the trusting spirit on,
  And bade it dwell with Uncreated Light.

Perchance when o'er thy loved paternal bower,
  The Sun of Righteousness shall healing rise,—
When India's children feel his noon-day power,
  And mingle all in Christian sympathies,—

Hither their pilgrim footsteps duly bound,
  With fervent zeal, these hallowed haunts shall trace,
And sweetly solemn tears bedew the ground
  Where sleeps the friend and prophet of their race !

A HYMN,

SUNG AT FINSBURY CHAPEL, MOORFIELDS, AFTER A FUNERAL SERMON

BY THE REV. W. J. FOX,

BY HARRIET MARTINEAU.

Music by Miss Flower.

No faithless tears, O God ! we shed
  For him who, to Thine altars led,
A swallow from a distant clime,
  Found rest beneath the cherubim ;
In Thee he rests from toil and pain,
  O Father ! hear our true Amen.

No faithless tears! Led forth by Thee,
Meek pilgrim to the sepulchre,
For him Thy truth from day to day,
Sprang up and blossomed by the way;
Shalt Thou not claim Thine own again?
O bend to hear deep Amen!

No faithless tears! Though many dream
To see his face by Ganges' stream;
Though thousands wait on many a shore,
The voice that shall be heard no more;
O, breathe Thy Peace amid their pain,
And hear Thy children's loud Amen!

SONNET

ON THE MEMORY

OF

THE RAJAH RAMMOHUN ROY.

WHEN from afar we saw thy burning light
Rise gloriously o'er India's darkened shore,
In spirit we rejoiced; and then still more
Rose high our admiration and delight,
When, steadfast to pursue thy course aright,
We saw thee brave fierce persecution's power.—
As yet we knew thee not,—but that blest hour
Which first disclosed thee to our longing sight,
Awakened in us deepest Christian love,
And told us thou hadst sat at Jesus' feet.
But now a glowing halo from above
Circles our thoughts of thee, when to the seat
Of mercy, rapt in ardent prayer, we come,
"Our Father! lead Thy wandering children home!"

M. C.

BRISTOL,
SUNDAY, *October 27th* 1833.

One other tribute remained to be paid to the remains of this great man. Sacred as was the spot where he was laid, and requiring to those who knew and loved him no stone to mark the spot, beneath the overhanging trees, which their hearts reverenced,—yet it was right that the public should have access to his grave, and should see a befitting monument erected over it. This could not be done at Stapleton Grove, which had now passed out of the CASTLE family. The Rajah's friend, the celebrated DWARKANATH TAGORE, desired to pay this mark of respect to his memory, and it was therefore arranged that the case containing the coffin should be removed to the beautiful cemetery of Arno's Vale, near Bristol. This was suitably accomplished on the 29th of May, 1843, and a handsome monument was erected in the spring of the year following by his friend, the enlightened and celebrated DWARKANATH TAGORE. * A visit was afterwards paid by him to the spot, and recently by his grandson, SATYENDRA NATH TAGORE.

DWARKANATH TAGORE died also in a strange land, but he lies in a gloomy cemetery in London, Kensal Green, and no tomb befitting his rank has been erected to mark the spot. Surely his remains

* A Half-tone picture of Prince Dwarkanath Tagore is given in this edition.

PRINCE DWARKA NATH TAGORE.

U. RAY & SONS

will be transferred to the spot where rests his noble friend !

Many of the countrymen † of the illustrious Brahmin have already visited the spot where reposes all of him that is mortal, and doubtless all will feel what is beautifully expressed by one of them,—"The place where lies the funeral temple of Rajah RAMMOHUN ROY is a sacred place for Hindoo Pilgrims !" May such a pilgrimage rouse and stimulate those who undertake it to fresh exertions for their country. "The memory of such a man," writes another, whose words have been already quoted in the preface, "must ever be dear to the Hindoos ; and it is the duty of those of our countrymen who can afford to visit England, not to return without paying their tribute of respect to the spot where rest the remains of that illustrious man. To perform this duty we have visited this famous city, which has the honour of possessing the mortal remains of RAMMOHUN ROY. It was the good name of your revered and pious father which brought the Rajah here, and it is that of the latter again which has attracted us here ; you can therefore imagine how greatly we must feel the satisfaction of having performed this pilgrimage (if I may so call it), with your

† A list of Indian gentlemen who visited the Raja's Tomb up to 1898 is given in appendix G.

kind assistance. We hope that the performance of this duty will stimulate our exertions, and help us on in following the paths of truth and righteousness. My great ambition in life is to be useful to my country, and to do good to others; it is this strong desire that has brought me to this part of the world, in order to seek knowledge; and the acquaintance of the great and the good. Our prayer is that God may give us the power, ability and knowledge, which we may devote to the service of our country. The performance of duty is its own reward, and though our exertions may not bear any fruit in our lifetime, the thought of having done our *duty* will be the greatest happiness to us. May God hasten the day when all strifes and party feelings will subside,—when sects and castes will merge into *one*, that of *humanity*,—when we shall cease to regard the English, the Hindoo, and the Jew, as belonging to defferent nations,—and when we shall all sing, the

"FATHERHOOD OF GOD AND BROTHERHOOD OF MAN."

Chapter V.

CONCLUSION.

It is probable that in many pulpits there were notices of the mournful event of the Rajah's death. The Rev. Dr. KENNEY, of St. Olave's Southwark, whose ministry RAMMOHUN ROY had frequently attended, preached a funeral sermon for him at the request of his parishioners; he also wrote a letter to Mr. J. HARE expressive of his warm attachment to the Rajah and high appreciation of his character. Five sermons were printed. In Lewin's mead Chapel, Bristol, where the Rajah had last worshipped. a funeral sermon was preached by Dr. CARPENTER to a densely crowded congregation on October 6th, 1833. It contains a full review of the labours, opinions and character of the Rajah, and was printed with a number of extracts from his writings, and with the Biographical Memoir at the commencement of this volume.

On the same Sunday, the Rev. R. ASPLAND

preached a funeral sermon in the New Gravel Pit Meeting, Hackney, where the Rajah had not unfrequently been a listener. A large portion of the semon consists of biographical notices of the Rajah, and extracts from his writings, which had been already presented to the public by Dr. CARPENTER. It was, therefore, not intended for publication. But an edition of the sermon having made its appearance (printed, it is supposed, from notes taken at the time of delivery), whitout the sanction of the author, no alternative was left to him, unless he could consent to bear the imputation of putting out a mean and illiterate publication, in reference to a name entitled to every outward mark of respect. On the title page of the sermon are the appropriate lines of the poet of Paradise Lost and Regained :—

> "One man except, the only son of light,
> In a dark age, against example good,
> Against allurement, custom, and a world
> Offended."

The subject of the sermon is "The future accession of good men of all climes to Christianity, and their final congregation in heaven." Mr. ASPLAND thus prefaced it,—

"Judging that it would not be uncongenial with the feelings of the congregation, nor presumptuous on my part, nor perhaps, wholly unserviceable to the cause of Christian truth, I ventured last Sunday morning to announce that I should adapt the present discourse to the melancholy event of the somewhat sudden and, according to the course of nature, premature decease of our distinguished oriental visitor, Rajah RAMMOHUN ROY; the rather, as he was an occasional worshipper in this House of Prayer, and repeatedly expressed that he felt a deep interest in this congregation. On that occasion, I stated that I did not meditate a mere eulogy upon the departed Brahmin. My object is to represent him as, with my means of knowledge, I consider him to have been, and to describe his religious character and profession as it appeared to myself, and to others that had still better means of forming a correct opinion. His condition in relation to Christianity was so peculiar; his rank and acquirements and labours justly attracted to him so much public attention; and so many contradictory statements have been made of his religious views, that it cannot be regarded as an indelicate or uninteresting inquiry, whether he embraced the gospel entirely and unreservedly, and what was his decision amidst the conflicting theories of Christian sects upon the true scheme of doctrine propounded in the Christian Scriptures."

Though the Rajah had not been able to visit

Ireland, yet the Sister Isle was not uninterested in the visit of the Hindoo Reformer, and on October 27th, 1833, a sermon was preached in the Presbyterian Church of Strand Street, Dublin, on the occasion of his death, by the Rev WILLIAM HAMILTON DRUMMOND, D. D., which was published by special request. "The Rajah received addresses", Dr. DRUMMOND states, "from Ireland, particularly from Belfast and Cork, and a gentleman of this city was commissioned by the Irish Unitarian Society to invite him to a public entertainment. It was accordingly his intention to pay this country a visit. He seemed to take a deep interest in the affairs of Ireland, and I can state on the unquestionable authority of a friend, who was frequently in his society in London, that in the course of a month after his arrival, he had acquired such an intimate knowledge of its statistics, politics and religion, as might almost justify the belief that he had long been directing his exclusive attention to those subjects of enquiry."

A funeral sermon on the death of the Rajah RAMMOHUN ROY, was also preached in the Meeting House of the first Presbyterian Congregation, Belfast, on Nov. the 10th, 1833 by the Rev. J. SCOTT PORTER. This gentleman was associated with Mr. DAVISON, when the Rajah confided to him the care of his adopted son, and there, he states, he had the high gratification and honour of forming the acquaintance of that illustrious man. Mr. PORTER had the privilege of being admitted to some degree of intimacy with the Rajah who seldom failed to call at least once a week to inquire respecting his son's progress. He had thus peculiar opportunities of acquiring a knowledge of the Rajah's manner and mind, as developed in ordinary intercourse. To these he bears strong testimony in the discourse.

The last sermon was by Rev. W. J. Fox, which he delivered in Finsbury Chapel, London. He concluded it with this eloquent tribute to the noble and beloved friend from the East, who had departed from among us. "We shall see his face no more! His presence has passed away as a poetic image fades from the brain! But it has left impressions which will long endure; influences of good, wide and deep, here; yet wider and deeper in the distant land of his nativity. And, 'being dead, he yet speaketh' with a voice to which not only India but Europe and America will listen for generations. A few days of fever have made him dust. It appears that no skill could have saved a life which, as he was probably but in about the fifty-fifth year of his age, seems to us prematurely terminated. Subsequent to all other signs of consciousness, he indicated the yet surviving sense of the kindness of his friends, and, by silent devotion of the presence of his God. His body will be silently committed to its rest in ground only hallowed by its reception—the noblest of all consecrations. Many will there be whom personal attachment will draw towards that spot, and it *should* draw them thither; for it is good to weep over the grave of such a man, and makes the heart better. Good will it be for them, there, to adopt as the rule of their own conduct his favourite quotation from the Persian poet, which he often wished should be inscribed on his tomb—'THE TRUE WAY OF SERVING GOD, IS TO DO GOOD TO MAN.'

"And if we shed at his death 'no faithless tears,' such is the service which the contemplation of his life will stimulate us to render. God is not served by our forms and ceremonies, our creeds and anathemas, our wild emotions, or our bustling zeal. He will have mercy, and not sacrifice. The garland with which the Hindoo decks his idol is not less worthy heaven than the useless observances and mysterious dogmas, by the faith and practice of which many who are called Christians, have thought to propitiate God. The dissemination of knowledge, the mitigation of suffering, the prevention of oppression, the promotion of improvement, the diffusion of a beneficent piety,—these are God's work, for us, towards others; and they are all reflected upon ourselves in the building up of our own characters to intellectual and moral excellence. 'Speaking the trurh in love,' we shall best bear our own testimony, and prolong theirs who have joined the 'cloud of witnesses' that compass us about, as we 'run the race set before us, looking unto Jesus.' The voice of duty may not call us to quit either country or kindred; but our souls have their pilgrimage of faith to pursue, through varied trials, to our Father's house, in which there are many mansions, wherein ultimately shall be gathered together the whole family of heaven and earth. Already should our hearts feel the bond of that holy fraternity,—the love which never faileth, which never shall fail, in time or in eternity; for it is the essence and the influence of God, and 'he that loveth dwelleth in God, and God in him.'

"Thus may we anticipate, according to our usefulness and progress, acceptance in degree like that which awaited our departed visitant and friend. For may we not devoutly trust that the Great Master has received him with—'Well done, good and faithful servant, enter thou into the joy of thy Lord;' and that patriarchs and prophets, apostles and confessors, philosophers and reformers, the holy and illustrious of all times and countries, gathering round to greet a brother, have responded in gratulation, Amen even so, Lord Jesus;"

Here we bring to a conclusion the notices we have been able to collect of the last days in England of the illustrious Hindoo Reformer, the Rajah RAMMOHUN ROY,—a man who, though he was greatly admired and appreciated during his life by those who could discern even a small portion of his greatness, will perhaps be far better comprehended, and therefore exert a far wider influence over his countrymen, now that the time has removed some of the barriers which separated him from them during his lifetime. India will doubtless not much longer delay to prepare for him an enduring tribute of reverence and respect, as well as to perpetuate the history of his life for future generations. It is probable that the painting from which the frontispiece is copied is the best representation of his living form that exists;—while the bust taken after death preserves his actual form. Will the capital of his country long remain without the honour of possessing such a statue of him as may show to future generations the noble benefactor of his country? Ere all have passed away who personally knew him in India will not efforts be made to collect all that can be known respecting him into a complete and permanent Memoir?

There is, however, one further mark of respect due to this illustrious Reformer, which he would value more highly than any other.

We have seen how earnestly he laboured to disseminate the great truths which he had devoted his whole life to discover, and to present them to his countrymen for their serious consideration in a simple and popular form. To accomplish this he spared no expense, no time, no personal exertion. His unexpected, and, to our narrow view, premature summons to the other world, prevented his accomplishing all he had purposed in this respect. His works were never given to his countrymen and to the world in a connected series:—many of the books which he published are now out of print,* and it is probable that manuscripts of his may yet be discovered which he intended for publication, had not death arrested his hand.

* This defect has since then been removed by the publication of his works.

Let his countrymen undertake the sacred task of collecting and publishing in a complete and permanent form all his works, and of rendering those of them to which he attached the greatest importance acceptable to the public generally by being printed in a cheap and popular edition. Thus will the most enduring monument be raised to his memory! Thus may his high and excellent aspirations be enabled to kindle the hearts of generation after generation of his countrymen, and through them of countless multitudes. Listening with reverence to his voice, now speaking to them from the World of Spirits, may his countrymen be led on by him to a pure and holy religion, which will guide them in peace and happiness through this world, and prepare them for another and a better. And thus without distinction of country or clime, shall myriads bless the name of the first Hindoo Reformer, the Rajah RAMMOHUN ROY.

APPENDIX.

(A)

LIST OF THE WORKS OF THE RAJAH RAMMOHUN ROY, WHICH HAVE BEEN PUBLISHED IN ENGLAND.

(*From the Notes to Mr. Fox's Sermon.*)

1. The Precepts of Jesus the Guide to Peace and Happiness, extracted from the Books of the New Testament ascribed to the Four Evangelists to which are added the First and Second Appeal to the Christian Public, in reply to the Observations of Dr. MARSHMAN, of Serampore. London, 1823.

2. Final Appeal to the Christian Public in Defence of the "Precepts of Jesus." London, Hunter, 1823.

3. Translation of several principal Books, Passages, and Texts of the Veds, and of some Controversial Works in Brahminical Theology. London, Parbury, 1832,

This Collection contains the following Tracts, to the titles of which are affixed the dates of their (English) publication at Calcutta :—

Translation of an Abridgment of the Vedant, or Resolution of all the Veds ; the most celebrated and revered Work of Brahminical Theology ; establishing the Unity of the Supreme Being, and that He alone is the Object of Propitiation and Worship. 1816.

Translation of the Moonduk-Oopunishud of the Uthurvu Ved. 1819.

Translation of the Céna Upanished, one of the Chapters of the Sáma Véda. 1824.

Translation of the Kut'h-Oopunishud of the Ujoor-Ved.

Translation of the Ishopunishud, one of the Chapters of the Yajur Veda. 1816.

A Translation into English of a Sungskrit Tract, inculcating the Divine Worship; esteemed by those who believe in the Revelation of the Veds, as most appropriate to the Nature of the Supreme Being. 1827.

A Defence of Hindoo Theism, in reply to the Attack of an Advocate for Idolatry, at Madras. 1827.

A Second Defence of the monotheistical System of the Véds; in reply to an Apology for present State of Hindoo Worship, 1817.

An Apology for the Pursuit of Final Beatitude, independently of Brahminical Observances. 1820.

Translation of a Conference between an Advocate for, and an Opponent of the practice of burning Widows alive; from the original Bungla, 1818.

A Second Conference between an Advocate for, and an Opponent of, the practice of burning Widows alive. 1820.

Abstract of the Arguments regarding the Burning of Widows, considered as a Religious Rite. 1830.

Brief Remarks regarding Modern Encroachments on the Ancient Rights of Females, according to the Hindoo Law of Inheritance. 1822.

4. Essay on the Right of Hindoos over Ancestral Property according to the Law of Bengal. With an Appendix containing Letters on the Hindoo Law of Inheritance. Calcutta, 1830. London: Smith, Elder and Co. 1832.

5. Exposition of the Practical Operation of the Judicial

and Revenue Systems in India, and of the general Character and Condition of its Native Inhabitants, as submitted in Evidence to the Authorities in England. With Notes and Illustrations, Also, a brief Preliminary Sketch of the Ancient and Modern Boundaries, and of the History of that country. London: Smith. 1832.

6. Answers to Queries by the Rev. H. WARE, of Cambridge, U, S., printed in "Correspondence relative to the Prospects of Christianity, and the Means of promoting its Reception in India" London: C. Fox. 1825.

7. Translation of the Creed maintained by the Ancient Brahmins, as founded on the Sacred Authorities. Second Edition, reprinted from the Calcutta Edition. London: Nichols and Son, 1833; pp. 15.

He was also the author of an able Memorial to the Privy Council on behalf of the Native Press of India; of a Bengalee Grammar in the English language; and, probably, of various publications not known in this country. His early work, which was written in Persian, with a preface in Arabic, "Against the Idolatry of all Religions," has not, so far as is known to the writer of this note, appeared in the English language. Besides some portion of a Life of Mahomet, already referred to, mention is made by Mr. ARNOTT, in the "Athenæum," of supposed works in favour of monotheism, and also that "he prepared, while in England, various able Papers or Essays on the working of the Supreme Court of Calcutta, against the Salt Monopoly in India, &c., which have not been published." If his "Journal". have been regularly and fully kept, its appearance must excite a strong interest.

(8)

RAJAH RAM ROY.

The following account of this youth was received by Dr. CARPENTER in a letter from India in 1835:—You ask me to give you any corrections (of Dr. C's Sermon and Review) that may appear necessary. One has been suggested to me by his native friends, as desirable to be made for the sake of RAMMOHUN ROY's character. The boy RAJAH whom he took with him to England is not his son, not even an adopted son according to the Hindoo form of adoption; but a destitute orphan whom he was led by circumstances to protect and educate. I have a distinct recollection of the particular circumstance under which, he stated to me RAJAH came into his hands. And my recollection is confirmed by that of others. Mr. DICK, a civil servant of the Company, found the child helpless and forsaken at one of the fairs at Hurdwar, where from two to three hundred thousand people annually congregated. It is not known whether the parents were Hindoos or Mussulmans, nor whether the parents lost or forsook him; but Mr. DICK had him clothed and fed, and when he was under the necessity of leaving the country for the recovery of his health, he consulted with RAMMOHUN ROY how the child should be disposed of. I well recollect our late friend's benevolent exclamation: "When I saw an Englishman, a Christian, thus caring for the welfare of a poor orphan, could I, a native, hesitate to take him under my care, and provide for him?" Mr. DICK never returned to India, having died, I believe, on the passage to England, and the child remained with RAMMOHUN ROY, who became so fond of him, that I often thought, and sometimes said, that he injured him by excessive indulgence. RAJAH RAM ROY returned to India, and has since died.

(C)

Two letters occur in the "Memoirs of JEREMY BENTHAM, by Sir JOHN BOWRING, chap. XXIII., P. 7, and chap. XXV p. 59, in reference to RAMMOHUN ROY, containing Sir JOHN'S estimate of his character.

(D)

The following communication from an English Officer who had attained the age of eighty-four, shows how deep was the respect and admiration felt for RAMMOHUN ROY :—

"MOUNT AUBURN, CINCINNATI, U. S. *4th Jnue*, 1866. "To Miss MARY CARPENTER, Bristol, England.

"DEAR MADAM,—In the event of the address of this letter being sufficiently correct for it to reach you safely, it will doubtless much surprise you to receive such a communication from an utter stranger in so distant a land. The shortest way therefore, of explaining matters, will be to proceed at once to state that I am a veteran British Officer and an old and intimate friend of the late estimable Rajah RAMMOHUN ROY ; and that having lately accidentally observed in an American journal a notice, stating that Miss MARY CARPENTER has in preparation 'The Last Days of Rajah RAMMOHUN ROY, with a portrait and Illustrations, I could not help feeling irresistibly inclined to confer with the fair biographer, and to state that, if still in time, I might happily be able to contribute a few acceptable items towards so desirable an object, having known the Rajah well in India and had the pleasure of frequent visits from and correspondence with him, particularly while my Regiment (the 17th) was quartered in Fort William, at Calcutta ; and having afterwards had the great satisfaction of meeting him in London, before he went into Somersetshire and was even led to hope that he would pay me a friendly visit in Devonshire, to which pleasant county I had then retired, and (as I thought settled down, with a rising family, for the remainder of my life. But, alas, though 'man may propose, it is God alone who disposes'—for we never met again; and not long after the Rajah's lamented death, I was from pecuniary reverses led, in 1836, to emigrate to Canada, in which colony I continued to reside for twenty years, when I was reluctantly induced to bid adieu to British soil, and take up my abode in this city to be near a beloved married daughter—now no more—and where I have resided ever since.

"Having taken a rapid retrospective glance through an eventful vista of more than forty years, I now return to the particular object in view, by mentioning as above observed, that I had the pleasure of knowing RAMMOHUN rather intimately in India, and that not only was I one of the particular friends invited to the great dinner given by him in honour of the supposed Revolution in Spain ; but he was even my guest at the Regimental mess table, in the Garrison of Fort William,—a very unusual thing in those days for a native gentleman, and more particularly a Brahmin ; and further that after my return to Europe, happening to visit Paris, I had the pleasure of being deputed by the *Societé Asiatique*, to forward to RAMMOHUN a Diploma of honorary membership of that learned and scientific body, long before such honorable notice had begun to be taken of him either in India or England ; and this Diploma was delivered to him by a mutual friend, whom I begged to inform me what effect this then unusal compliment appeared to produce on RAMMOHUN'S feelings,—and whose reply I still possess. I am also desirous of calling your attention to a particular circumstance connected with the defence of the fair fame and name of our deceased friend, in my having, shortly after his death been so incensed by some uncalled for sneers at his memory by a flippant Editor of the London *Times*, as to have, in November 1832, induced me to insert an indignant communication on the subject in the *Nāval and Militāry Gazette*, then edited by Mr. Montgomery Martin (also an intimate personal friend of the deceased) which, I became aware, cut to the quick.

"I could readily refer to other reminiscences ; but I deem the above sufficient at present ; and shall therefore be content to add that should this communication be thought worthy of an acknowledgment, letters addressd simply to Colonel LACHLAN, Cincinnati, Ohio, U. S. will be sure to find me ; and that I beg to be permitted to remain in the meantime,

"Dear Madam,

"Yours most respectfully and sincerely,

"R. LAGHLAN."

(E)

REMINISCENCES OF RAJAH RAMMOHUN ROY.

WRITTEN BY A HINDOO GENTLEMAN.

"My father and Rajah RAMMOHUN ROY were friends. The friendship arose from the circumstance of their mofussil residence being in the same part of the district of Hooghly. My father was an orthodox Brahmin, but this did not interrupt his friendship with the old Rajah when his heterodoxy came to light, for, though of the class, my father was liberal and had a great respect for the Rajah. So great was his attachment to his noble friend that he well nigh suffered excommunication for it, when the abolition of suttee brought upon the Rajah, as the author of this outrage, that social misfortune.

"I was introduced to the Rajah at a very early age by my father, and the friendship of the fathers soon led to the establishment of a friendship between the sons. The Rajah's youngest son, the late ROMA PERSHAD ROY, and I being nearly of the same age, and being consequently thrown into each other's society, we soon began to find a pleasure in being together, and our intimacy grew up with our years. We lived like brothers, and the friendly relations between our families were gradually firmly cemented.

"Not long after I had been established in the family of the Rajah, the Rev. Dr. DUFF whose memory I cannot recall without a thrill of gratitude passing through my frame, came to India and formed a project in concert with the Rajah of establishing a school for giving English education to native children. At that time, missionaries and missionary institutions were regarded by natives with great mistrust, and the Doctor and the Rajah with great difficulty could obtain but five pupils for their projected new school. I was one of these five, and I am now the only survivor out of this lot. The good Doctor has mentioned this fact with great complacency in many of his recent discourses both here and in Edinburgh.

"My friend, ROMA PERSHAD, and I formed, as far back as 1860, a scheme of giving instruction to the females of respectable Hindoo families. The system of Zenana teaching which then came into existence was to our minds not suited to this end and we arranged for instructing our females in some respectable school, to be established in the heart of the native town, presided over and managed by some respectable mistress, respectable not only in attainments but also in social position. We broached our scheme to Dr. DUFF, who approved of it fully, and engaged the services of a clergyman's wife for this purpose in England. But before we could carry our scheme into operation, I was deputed by Government to Lahore on public duty, and during my absence there my friend was gathered to his fathers, and our cherished scheme fell to the ground.

"The untimely death of my lamented friend rendered abortive several other schemes that we fondly cherished. Among other things we had an idea of going to England together, there to visit the place where his illustrious father sojourned and breathed his last, and ultimately to erect a marble statue on the spot to preserve his memory ; but the hand of death anticipated us, and the regret is that we fell short of our duty to the illustrious deceased, not that his memory will be lost, for it requires no artificial monument to preserve it, and even if it does there is a more substantial monument which will last so long as the English literature endureth, "K. M. CHATTERJEE.

"*Calcutta, 22nd Dec., 1866*"

(F)

THE RAJAH'S TOMB IN ARNO'S VALE CEMETERY.

In 1872 the tomb was put into beautiful repair at the expense of the executors of the Rajah, and the following inscripton has been carved on it at their desire :—

Beneath this stone
rest the remains of Rajá Rammohun Roy Bahadoor,
a conscientious and steadfast believer in the Unity of the Godhead
he consecrated his life with entire devotion
to the worship of the DIVINE SPIRIT alone.

To great natural talents he united thorough mastery of many languages, and early distinguished himself as one of the greatest scholars of his day.

His unwearied labours to promote the social, moral and physical condition of the people of India, his earnest endeavours to suppress idolatry and the rite of Suttee, and his constant zealous advocacy of whatever tended to advance the glory of God and the welfare of man live in the grateful remembrance of his countrymen.

This tablet records the sorrow and pride with which his memory is cherished by his descendants.

He was born at Radhanagore, in Bengal, in 1774. and died at Bristol, September 27th, 1833.

(G)

ARNO'S VALE CEMETERY.

THE HOMAGE BY INDIAN VISITORS.

THE LAST RESTING PLACE OF THE MORTAL REMAINS OF RAJA RAMMOHUN ROY.

A young friend who was studying in England in 1898 sent the following intersting account of his pilgrimage to the Sacred Remains of the RAJAH RAMMOHUN ROY at Bristol. We present our readers with the contents of the 'Visitor's Book' kept at the Cemetery as taken down on the 11th of September, 1898.

"The book begins by saying how at the wish of the grandson of the Raja, Mr. Kishori Mohan Chattopadhyay (late Judge S. C. Court, Calcutta), this book was begun on the 8th October, 1869. This is in the handwriting of Miss Mary Carpenter, who puts in a note in one of the pages that "the spot where he was first laid is marked by some pieces of granite") i.e., in Stapleton Grove".

Then follow names of gentlemen who had visited the grove before the book was started. The names are :—Jagat Chandra Ganguly, (a Christian) 1860 ; Rakhal Das Haldar, 1861 ; Satyendra Nath Tagore and Manomohun Ghosh, Calcutta 1863 ; Ram Chandra Balkrishna (Bombay) 1865 ; Karan Das Mulji, (Bombay) 1867 ; Womesh Chandra Banerjee ; Khetra Mohun Dutt, (Medical Practitioner), and Monomohun Ghosh, December, 1864.

Then follow names and remarks written by visitors themselves. Kishori Mohun Chattopadhyay, October 2nd, 1869 ; Surendra Nath Banerjee (same date) ;

Then the following :—

"Keshub Chunder Sen,. left Calcutta on Tuesday, February 15th, arrived in London on Monday, March 21st, and visited RAJAH RAM-MOHUN ROY'S Tomb at Arno s Vale Cemetery on Sunday, June 12th, 1870. "May the Lord bless his soul."

Rakhal Chandra Roy (same date) May God have mercy on his soul."

"Prosonno Coomar Sen, 15th June, 1870. "May the Lord bless his soul."

Then follow :—

"Kazi Shahabuddin and G. A. Daphtary, 23rd, July 1870.

"Anandamohan Bose, of Bengal, visited the Tomb which makes the Cemetry an object of deep and solemn interest to an Indian heart, on the 10th September, 1870. "May those who come here carry back with them some of that spirit which animated the Rajah, and made him a Morning Star of Reform in his native land."

Krishna Gopal Deshmukh, 12th April, 1871; Sasipada Banerjea, 7th July, 1871; Dr. Gopal Chandra Roy, 7th July 1871; Radhika Prosad Ghosh, 22nd June 1872; Dr. Charles Stras Burges of Warsaw (Poland), 16th July 1872; Dr. Guillamma Neuchatel (Switzerland) 16th July, 1872; Krishna Gopal Deshmukh, 26th January, 1873. C. Menacshaya of Madras, and C. Sobha Patti Iyalis, 21st Sept 1873; Miss Harriet Ware of Boston, November 19th 1873; Nanaji Narayan of Bombay 11th July 1874.

"Protap Chunder Mozoomdar of Calcutta, a missionary of the Brahmo Somaj of India, the church for the worship of one God, which the Rajah founded in the year 1831, and which makes his name immortal in the ancient land of his birth, visited this cemetery on the 19th July 1874. "England for ever will remain a land of pilgrimage to every patriotic and pious Hindu, so long as the Sacred Remains of our beloved Rajah lie enshrined in her free soil, and if, in the course of time, all other relations that bind India and the land of her rulers come to be loosened and ineffective, this shall for ever unite the two countries which represent the East and the West, that the last days—the noblest days of RAJAH RAMMOHUN ROY—were spent, and the last efforts of his great soul were made in England, after he had successfully established in his fatherland the institution which proposes itself the object of introducing into the world the Fatherhood of God and Brotherhood of Man. May others be inspird as I have been by the sight of the Rajah's grave."e

Pakula Venkata Krishnan Naidu (Madras), August 2nd, 1874; Palicat Ratnu Melu Chetty (same date); Avinash Chandra Mitra, December 18th 1874; Kavarji Mervunji Shroff, January 7th, 1875; Srinath Dutt, July 18th 1875. J. N. Sircar, B. D. Bose and W. M. Das, 18th August 1876; Mr and Mrs Turkeed (of Bombay), August 26th 1876, Satya Prokash Banerji, June 30th 1877; Rev. William Thomas Satthianadham (Chaplain to the Bishop of Madras) with Lord Bishop Anderson, June 21st 1878; Rama Bai Medhabi, May 9th 1885—with four lines in Marhatti, which translate thus:—

"Looking at the Samadhi of our great friend, who strove for our good, I felt both joy and sorrow; but I am happy, for the soul of the RAJAH RAMMOHUN ROY exists in the Infinite bliss of God".

K. B. Todhabu Baneryea, June 3rd 1886; Nitya Gopal Mukherjea (same date); T. N.

Mukherji, September 8th, 1886. Sivanath Sastri; Satis Ranjan Das; Durga Mohun Das; May 19th, 1888,

"Sivanath Sastri, September 27th 1888. "To day is the Anniversary of the death of RAJA RAMMOHUN ROY. I paid a second visit to his tomb this day. I thank God that we have succeeded in repairing his tomb during the interval and after our arrival in this country. The grandsons of the Rajah have promised to bear the cost of the repairs, which is £ 30 of English money, and I hope they will do so. If not, the Brahmos of Bengal will willingly bear it. I prayed this day by the side of the tomb, that this noble example may inspire us to follow in the same path."

"Rukma Bai (Bombay). July 10th 1890, with three or four lines in Mahratti, which translate :—May the soul of the noble RAJAH RAMMOHUN ROY, who devoted his life for the welfare of Indian women, be in peace".

Chandra Sekhar Sen, August 8th 1890; Tej Narain Singh (of Bhagalpur) and Syed Humayun Mirza, of Patna May 17th 1892; Albion R. K. Banerji, September 6th 1893; Bemal Chandra Ghosh and myself on Septemder 11th 1898.

After more than five years of no visitors we had gone to ask for the book; well might old Mr Henry I. Fentham (the Record-Keeper) remark that for a long time no one had used it. We took down some of the remarks that day, and returned three or four days later with a few other friends, once more to pay our tribute of respect to that great man. May our pilgrimage bless us with its grace.

(H)

A SHORT BIOGRAPHY OF THE LATE MISS MARY CARPENTER.

BY

Mr. D. N. PAL.

The 3rd April 1807, the birthday of MARY CARPENTER—was indeed a remarkable day. Her Life was of a farreaching usefulness. Her philanthropic labours are well known, and must be known to all readers of social reform movements. The events of her career are depicted in her books, her papers, and her Institutions such as the Ragged School and the Reformatory and Industrial Schools. These last were certainly the readiest means of ameliorating the condition of the outcast and the destitute whose wretched habit and despicable characrter shocked the heart of the philanthropic lady. She brought her powerful intellect to bear upon the unformed minds with which she daily came in contact. She possessed wonderful qualities of both head and heart,—qualities very rarely found in harmonious combination in the same individual. She had the insight into affairs and the grasp of detail of a born administrator. Under her vigillant and affectionate care, hundreds of souls have been rescued from the hanuts of poverty and crime. One cannot too much admire the remarkble sagacity and uncommon sympathy, displayed by her in dealing with the problem of ragged delinquency. Along with the foundation of the National Indian Association, the late MARY CARPENTER started a monthly, under the name of the *Journal of The National Indian Association*, as a medium for supplying information .on social matters and solution of important social questions. Until her death, she was the Editor of this Journal.

The influence of RAJAH RAMMOHUN ROY awakened her interest in the Indian people which soon developed itself into warm sympathy. Subsequently her conversation with the Rajah who visited her, resulted in the conviction that there was a vast field of philanthropic enterprise awaiting any one who would go to India without prejudice ; and she determined to enter upon it at once. She sailed for India in her sixtieth year, with a weak constitution and with no relative or friend accompanying her. Her only desire was to work in this country, under the stimulus which she received from the the RAJAH. During her sojourn, female education, reformatory schools, and the state of the jails engrossed all her attention. She was surprised to see that the classes in the girl's schools were conducted by male teachers. She felt this as a serious obstacle in the cause of female education. She did much to create public opinion in regard to the urgent need of gradually introducing trained female teachers into the schools. When the want of trained female teachers was universally felt in India she sought the co-operation of Government in this matter. At her request, Government took the initiative in founding schools for the training of female teachers. In the Presidency Towns, Female Normal Schools came to be thus established. But in Calcutta the School was abolished after nearly a year's trial for want of adequate support.

The efforts of Mary Carpenter in, Calcutta awakened an enthusiasm for social refrom. The Bengal Social Science Association was formally inaugurated. A constitution for the Society was drawn up. However, when she turned her back upon India, the Association died a premature death. The Bengal Branch of the National Indian Association was established in 1876, Babu Sasipada Banerji had some hand in it and framed rules for the society. The Branch Association was opened on the 11th April, under the presidency of Sir Richard Temple. Mrs. Sale and Mrs. P. L. Roy were Joint Secretaries.

Mr. Sasipada Benerji of the DEVALAYA with his wife accampanied Miss CARPENTER to England and spent about 9 months in her house near Bristol and it was here that his son Mr. ALBION BANERJI, M. A., I. C. S., (Dewan of Cochin) was born. Miss CARPENTER visited India 4 times on her educational and philanthropic mission. During her last trip to India she was much pleased to see the marked improvements effected in the condition of the women of this country. During this time she also visited the various important places of India and submitted an exhaustive report to Lord Salsbury, the then Prime Minister of England, on female education and the condition of the prisoners in the Indian Jails as a result of which this question was actively taken up by the Parliament and the Government of India passed an Act in 1876 for the Establishment of Reformatory Schools. The remarkable improvements in the condition of the Indian prisoners which we now notice in the Jails are due to a large extent to the indefatigable labours of Miss CARPENTER.

Mary CARPENTER died at Bristol on the 15th June 1877, at the age of 70. Her death was a sudden one. Four months after this lamentable event, a public meeting was held in the Guild Hall at Bristol at which it was resolved to perpetuate the memory of the late Miss Mary CARPENTER by the promotion of some philanthropic works in which she took particular interest. An Association was formed for the establishment and support of houses bearing her name for working boys, and working women and girls. The "MARY CARPENTER HALL" attached to the Brahmo Girls School in Circular Road and close to the Rammohun Memorial Hall and Library is another of her Memorials in Calcutta. Great credit is due to the members of the Brahmo Somaj for erecting this Memorial and associating her name with a cause with which she was so intimately connected during her life time.

At the invitation of the Dean who was her friend, a monument was placed in the wall of the Bristol Cathedral and we think we cannot do better than give a verbatim copy of what is inscribed on that tablet which was composed by the late Revd. Dr. Martineau,—

"SACRED TO THE MEMORY OF MARY CARPENTER,

Foremost among the founders of Reformatory and Industrial Schools in this city and realm.

Neither the claims of private duty nor the tastes of a cultured mind could withdraw her compassionate eye from the uncared for children of the streets.

Loving them while yet unlovely,
she so formed them to the fair and good
as to inspire others with her faith and hope,
and thus led the way to a National system
of moral rescue and preventive discipline.

Taking also to heart the grevious lot of oriental women, in the last decade of her life, she four times went to India,

and awakened an active interest
in their education and training for various duties.

No human ill escaped her pity, or cast down her trust, with true self secrifice she followed in the train of Christ, to seek and to save that which was lost and bring it home to the father-in-heaven.

Desiring to extend her work of piety and love
many who honoured her have instituted in
her name, some homes for the houseless young,
and now complete their tribute of affection
by erecting this memorial."

Born at Exeter— April 3rd. 1807.
Died at Bristol—June 15th. 1877.

APPENDIX I.

RAMMOHUN ROY.*

The Last Days in England of the Rajah Rammohun Roy. Edited by Mary Carpenter of Bristol., London, Trübner & Co., Paternoster Row. 1866.

THE appearance of this work is very opportune. At a time when the Brahmo Somaj is rent by schism, and its conservative and progessive elements are struggling for mastery, the question as to what were the real religious opinions of its founder, has acquired a new interest, and demands a satisfactory solution.*

The most interesting portion of the work under review is that which furnishes us with materials for discussing that question, albeit the authoress herself does not grasp it with that perspicuity and impartiality which one in her position might be expected to bear on it. We shall not, therefore,

* This criticism appeared in the Calcutta Review, 1866.

hesitate to make such use of them as may be necessary for our purpose. Although not an original or independent work, yet as a compilation of various documents, letters, and accounts, her work is valuable, and will prove a great help to the future biographer of Rammohun Roy.

The first chapter of Miss Carpenter's work gives a biographical sketch of Rammohun Roy, but it is destitute of anecdotal and personal interest. It relates very little of his antecedents, and gives but an imperfect picture of his early career. In No. VIII, Vol. IV. of the *Calcutta Review*, the writer of this paper endeavoured to give an account of the parentage, education, and labours of the great Hindu, and he does not, therefore, think it necessary to reproduce it here. We have perhaps no right to find fault with the authoress for skipping over the early part of his career, inasmuch as the task she proposed to herself, namely, to describe the last days of the Hindu Reformer, has been very fairly performed. Indeed, the performance does credit both to her head and heart, and entitles her to the gratitude of all—and their number is legion—to whom the subject is congenial. The last days of Rammohun Roy, embracing as they do, his short but eventful career in Europe and evolution of his religious and political proclivities, are indeed fraught with an abiding interest to the natives of India, not less than to those Englishmen who profess something more than a mere personal interest in the progress and welfare of Hindustan.

Rammohun Roy was in the land of his birth, as Miss Carpenter justly observes, a man greatly before his age, and a light shining in thick and impenetrable darkness. Endowed with a bold spirit and a penetrating genius he could not long have remained among the myriad millions who live and die in nominal belief but whose religion is really regulated by the geography of their country or the prejudices of their nursery. Hence, while he was appreciated only by the little band of followers, whom he had enlisted in the cause of religious reform, he was denounced and persecuted by the mass of his countrymen. Born and bred in a country immersed in the darkness of superstition, he, by a proper use of his cultivated understanding, discovered the falsity of Hinduism, publicly renounced it, embraced theism, and thereby subjected himself to those terrors of excommunication, of which we can have a faint idea in this age of comparative enlightenment. He was a *melacha* and a *nastic* —an infidel and an arch-preacher of infidelity and as such to be cast aside with one general mark of reprobation. Persecuted at home, he turned to England for encouragement, sympathy, and help, for Englishmen had evinced a keen appreciation of his unselfish devotion to the highest interest of his countrymen. He longed to see the country to whose keeping the destinies of his own had been entrusted,—the country, where philosophy, liberty, and science had achieved their proudest triumphs,—the country of the Lockes, of the Bacons, of the Newtons, of the Hampdons, and of the Watts. By this visit to England he proposed to attain two objects,—first, to obtain, as he says in one of his letters, "by personal observa- " tion a more thorough insight into its manners, " customs, religion, and political institutions ;" and, secondly, to seek for help in his efforts to regenerate his fatherland. Without further preface we will now follow Miss Carpenter in her account of the pilgrimage to England of this adventurous enquirer after truth.

"The arrival of the illustrious Hindu Reformer

"to our country was anxiously anticipated by "all who had become acquainted with him through "the various channels which have been laid before "the reader. The nature of his labours, and the "distance of the scene of them, naturally prevented "his being an object of popular enthusiasm ;—nor, "if that had been excited in his favour, would he "have desired the public demonstrations of admira-"tion and respect which were recently accorded "to the great Italian patriot. But the reception "given to him, though of a widely different kind "must have been no less gratifying to him at the "time, and to his countrymen since his departure. "The highest honours were publicly accorded to "him, and a place was awarded to him among the "foreign ambassadors at the coronation of the "sovereign ; persons the most remarkable for their "social standing and literary eminence sought "his society, and highly esteemed the privilege "of intercourse with him ;—he was received into "our English homes not only as a distinguished "guest, but as a friend ;—and when he was pros-"trated on the bed of sickness and of death in "a foreign land, he was surrounded with the most "loving attentions, tended with the most anxious "solicitude, and finally laid in the grave surround-"ed with true mourners, who felt him akin to "them in spirit, if not connected with him by the "ties of earthly relationship."

The *Albion* in which he sailed arrived at her destination on the 8th April, 1831. The Rajah landed the same day at Liverpool, and took up his lodging at one of the hotels there. His arrival in England, where his fame had preceded him, excited a considerable degree of interest. It occurred too, at a period of extraordinary fermentation. The whole nation had been wrought up into a state of overpowering excitement. Reform was then, as it is now, the one great subject which agitated the whole country. Rammohun Roy became a zealous and enthusiastic advocate of "the Bill." He saw at once the good which this great national measure was calculated, in his opinion, to accomplish. He was convinced that it was calculated to "promote the welfare of England " and her dependencies —nay, of the whole world." It was under the hospitable roof of Mr. William Rathbone that he met the venerable Mr. Roscoe his first interview with whom is thus related :—"After the usual gesture of eastern salutation, and with a " mixture of oriental expression, Rammohun " Roy said, 'Happy and proud am I—proud " 'and happy to behold a man whose fame " 'has extended not only over Europe, but " 'over every part of the world.' 'I bless " 'God,' replied Mr. Roscoe, 'that I have been " 'permitted to live to see this day.'" Their " 'conversation chiefly turned upon the objects which had led Rammohun Roy to England and in the course of it he displayed an intimate acquaintance with the political and commercial state of that country.

The visit of the Rajah to Liverpool was a very short one from his anxiety to be present at the third reading of the Reform Bill, and at the debates on the subject of India. On his departure for London he carried with him the following letter from Mr. Roscoe to Lord Brougham :—

"I have the great honour and very singular " pleasure of introducing to your Lordship's kind " notice and attention the bearer of this, the " celebrated and learned Rammohun Roy, who is "just arrived here from Calcutta, and of whom "you must already have frequently heard as the "illustrious convert from Hindooism to Christian-"ity, and the author of the 'Selections from the "New Testament' and of 'The Precepts of Jesus' "by the publication and diffusion of which amongst "the natives of the East reasonable hopes are now "entertained, that, in a short time, the shocking "system and cruel practices of Paganism will be "abolished, and the people of those populous "regions be restored to the pure and simple "precepts of morality and brotherly love. Amongst "the many and important motives which have "induced him to leave his country and connections, "and visit this Island, I understand he is induced "to hope he may be of some assistance in promoting "the cause of the natives of India in the great "debates which must ere long take place here, "respecting the charter of the East India "Company; but I have yet seen so little of him, "from his numerous engagements here, that "I must leave your Lordship to learn his inten-"tions from himself, which you will find him "very capable of explaining in his own strong "and appropriate English idiom. One great "reason, as I understand, for his haste to leave "this for London, is to be present to witness the "great measures that will be taken by your Lord-"ship and your illustrious colleagues for promo-"ting the long wished for reform of his native coun-"try. On the present occasion, I will not trouble you "further than to request, that, if it should not be "inconsistent with your Lordship's station and "convenience, you would obtain for our distinguish-"ed visitor the benefit of a seat under the gallery "in the House of Commons, on the debate on "the third reading of the Reform Bill; which

" favour I am anxious he should owe rather to " your Lordship (if you have no objection to it) " than to other idividuals, to whom, I understand, " he has letters of introduction."

The purity and loftiness of his religious ideas and his freedom from sectarianism endeared Rammohun Roy to a large section of Christians in England,who eagerly sought to do him honour. He was warmly welcomed by them as a fellow-labourer and received by them with every mark of deep and heartfelt respect. Soon after his arrival in London, he attended a meeting of the Unitarian Society, convened to give him a welcome. On his appearance on the platform, he was introduced as the "Apostle of the East," and was thus cordially greeted by the Reverend Robert Aspland, who presided on the occasion. "Our illustrious friend (for " such I trust he will allow me to call him) will " permit me to state that his presence creates among " us a sensation which he perhaps will hardly under- " stand. It does so, because in his person and " example we see an instance of the power of the " human mind in recovering itself from the errors " of ages ; and because so we conceive that we " see in him, with his intelligence and character, " one of the best and most disinterested of the " claims of Unitarianism to be the original Christian " doctrine."

Dr. Bowring (now Sir John Bowring) in moving the resolution tendering a cordial welcome to the Hindu Reformer made the following pertinent remarks :—

"I feel it is a very signal honour to have entrus- "ed to my care a resolution, the object of which "is to welcome our illustrious oriental friend, and " to communicate all we feel and hope towards " him. I ought not to say all we feel and hope,

"for I am sure that it is impossible to give ex-
"pression to those sentiments of interest and
"anticipation with which his advent here is as-
"sociated in all our minds. I recollect some
"writers have indulged themselves with inquiring
"what they should feel if any of those time-
"honoured men whose names have lived through
"the vicissitudes of ages, should appear among
"them. They have endeavoured to imagine what
"would be their sensations if a Plato or a Socrates,
"a Milton or a Newton, were unexpectedly to
"honour them with their presence. I recollect
"that a poet, who has well been called divine,
"has drawn a beautiful picture of the feelings of
"those who first visited the Southern Hemisphere,
"and there saw, for the first time, that beautiful
"constellation, the Golden Cross. It was with
"feelings, such as they underwent, that I was
"overwhelmed when I stretched out in your name
"the hand of welcome to the Rajah Rammohun
"Roy. In my mind the effect of distance is very
"like the effect of time, and he who comes among
"us from a country thousands of miles off, must
"be looked upon with the same interest as those
"illustrious men who lived thousands of years ago.
"But in the case of our friend, his coming may be
"deemed an act of heroism of which the European
"cannot form a just estimate. When Peter the
"Great went forth to instruct himself in the
"civilization of the South,—when he left the
"barbarous honours of his own court to perfect
"himself in ship-building at Sardam,he presented
"himself to public eye in a more illustrious
"manner than after any of his most glorious
"victories. But Peter had to overcome no pre-
"judices, he had to break down no embarrass-
"ments, for he knew that he had left those who

"were behind him with an enthusiasm equal to "his own, and he knew that he would be received "by them, when he should return, with the same "display of enthusiasm. Our illustrious friend, "however, has made a more severe experiment: "he has ventured to accomplish that which "perhaps none other connected, as he is, with "the highest honours of the Brahminical race "ever attempted: he has ventured to do that "which would have been regarded with incredulity "ten years ago and which hereafter will crown "his name with the highest honour.

"Sir, I move with great pleasure, 'That the "'members of this Assciation feel a deep interest "'in the amelioration of the condition of the "'natives of British India; that we trust their "'welfare and imporvement will never be lost "'sight of by the Legislature and Government "'of our country; that we have special pleasure "'in the hope that juster notions and purer forms "'of religion are gradually advancing amongst "'them; and that our illustrious visitor from "'that distant region, the Rajah Rammohun Roy, "'be hereby certified of our sympathy in his "'arduous and philanthrophic labours, of our "'admiration of his character, of our delight at "'his presence amongst us, and of our conviction "'that the magnanimous and beneficent course "'which he has marked out for himself and "'hitherto consistently pursued, will entitle him "'to the blessings of his countrymen and of man- "'kind, as it will assuredly receive those of future "'generations.'"

Dr. Kirkland, late President of Harvard University, United States, seconded the resolution. In adopting it, the assembly rose in unanimous approbation of its object.

Rammohun Roy acknowledged the compliment in the following memorable terms :—"I am too unwell and too much exhausted to take any active "part in this meeting.; but I am much indebted "to Dr. Kirkland and to Dr. Bowring for the "honour they have conferred on me by calling me "their fellow-labourer, and to you for admitting "me to this Society as a brother and one of your "fellow-labourers. I am not sensible that I have "done anything to deserve being called a promoter "of this cause ; but with respect to your faith "I may observe, that I too believe in the one "God, and that I believe in almost all the doc-"trines that you do : but I do this for my own "salvation and for my own peace. For the "objects of your Society I must confess that "I have done very little to entitle me to your "gratitude or such admiration of my conduct. "What have I done ?—I do not know what "have I done !—If I have rendered you any "services they must be very trifling—very trifling "I am sure, I laboured under many disadvantages. "In the first instance, the Hindus and the Brah-"mins, to whom I am related, are all hostile to "the cause ; and even many Christians there "are more hostile to our common cause than the "Hindus and the Brahmins. I have honour for "the appellation of Christians ; but they always "tried to throw dificulties and obstacles in the "way of the Principles of Unitarian Christianity. I "have found some of these here ; but more there. "They abhor the notion of simple precepts. They "always lay a stress on mystery and mystical "points, which serve to delude their followers ; "and the consequence is, that we meet with such "opposition in India that our progress is very "slight ; and I feel ashamed on my side that I "have not made any progress, that might have "placed me on a footing with my fellow-labourers "in this part of the globe. However, if this is "the true system of Christianity, it will prevail, "notwithstanding all the opposition that may be "made to it. Scripture seconds your system of "religion, common sense is always on your side; "while power and prejudice are on the side of your "opponents. There is a battle going on between "reason, Scripture, and common sense; and "wealth, power, and prejudice. These three "have been struggling with the other three, but I "am convinced that your success, sooner or later "is certain. I feel overexhausted, and therefore "conclude with an expression of my heart-felt "thanks for the honour that, from time to time you "have conferred on me, and which I shall never "forget to the last moment of my existence."

The religious sympathy evinced towards Rammohun Roy by the Unitarians of England must have been refreshing to his spirit, and compensated in no inconsidarable degree for the persecutions to which he had been subjected in India. "While in London," says "Dr. Carpenter, "he repeatedly attended the "worship of the Unitarians, at their different "chapels in or near the metropolis, and he twice "attended their anniversary meetings: but it was "his system to avoid so far identifying himself "with any religious body, as to make himself "answerable for their acts and opinions; and he "also wished to hear preachers of other denomina- "tions who had acquired a just celebrity. He "appears to have most frequented the church of "the Rev. Dr. Kenny (St. Olave's Southwark), "who peculiarly interested him by the Christian "spirit and influence of his discourses.

While in London, Rammohun Roy had the satisfaction of seeing the appeal of the *Dharma-sabha* against Lord William Bentinck's edict for the abolition of *Suttee* rejected by the Privy Council, and the Charter Act for India passed by the Parliament. As a patriot and a politician he rejoiced in these measures, for he was both in the truest sense of those words and needed but a larger stage to rank in sober reality with the foremost statesmen of the age.

It was however as a philosopher and a reformer that he was sought after and prized by intellectual and thoughtful men in England. The following interesting anecdotes illustrate his views on philosophical and religious subjects. The first is from the pen of Mr. Recorder Hill :—"I only met "the Rajah Rammohun Roy once in my life. It was " at a dinner party given by Dr. Arnott. One of " the guests was Robert Owen, who evinced a " strong desire to bring over the Rajah to his " socialistic opinions. He persevered with great " earnestness, but the Rajah who seemed well-" acquainted with the subject, and who spoke our " language in marvellous perfection, answered " his arguments with consummate skill, until " Robert somewhat lost his temper, a very rare " occurrence, which I never witnessed before. The " defeat of the kind-hearted philanthropist was " accomplished with great suavity on the part of " his opponent."

The next is from a lady acquaintance of theRajah :-

" At a small evening party at my house in " Grenville Street, principally to meet the Rajah, " he referred to the doctrine of Original Sin in a " way that startled a lady of the Church—a very " charming and amiable woman,—who had brought " her daughter. 'But surely, Sir,' she exclaimed, "you do believe in Original Sin ?' He looked at "her and she blushed deeply. After a minute, he "seemed to comprehend the whole, and very "gently inclining he said, 'I believe it is a doctrine "which in many well-regulated minds has tended "to promote humility, the first of Christian "virtues; for my own part, I have never been "able to see the evidence of it."

In compliance with the reiterated invitation of "Miss Kiddell, Rammohun Roy went to Bristol "early in the month of September, 1833. He "put up at Stapleton Grove, the residence of Miss "Kiddell and her ward Miss Catherine Cassell. "He was accompanied by Miss Hare the niece, and "not, as Miss Carpenter supposes, the daughter of "David Hare, the father of native education in "Bengal; he was attended by his two Hindu ser-"vants, Ramrutton Mookerjee, afterwards Deputy Collector of Moorshedabad, and now residing at Maniktollah; and Ramhurry Doss, now Head Gardener of the Maharajah of Burdwan. The fame of the services rendered by the Hindu Reformer to the cause of Unitarian Christianity in India had preceded him in Bristol about eight years before his arrival there, when an appeal on behalf of that cause had been made to the congregation and had been responded to most liberally. It is, therefore, small wonder that his appearanace in Lewin's Mead Chapel was warmly welcomed. He visited also other places of worship, and while engaged in public devotion there he was wont to read some of Dr. Watts's hymns for children, and he frequently dwelt with great interest on the following verse:

"Lord! how delightful 'tis to see
"A whole assembly worship Thee:
"At once they sing, at once they pray;
"They hear of heaven and learn the way."

On the eleventh September of 1833, a large party was invited by Miss Kiddell to meet Rammohun Roy at Stapleton Grove. The conversation was animated and protracted and elicited the Rajah's various talents, breadth of view, and grasp of mind, calling forth the admiring respect of the company. It is thus described by Dr, Carpenter: "In the conversation at Stapleton "Grove were men fully competent to judge of "intellectual power; and one and all admired and "were delighted by the clearness, the closeness, "and the acuteness of his arguments, and the "beautiful tone of his mind. In the second of "of the two conversations at which Mr. Lister "was present, the Rajah continued for three hours, "standing the whole time, replying to all the "inquiries and observations that were made by a "number of gentlemen who surrounded him, on "the moral and political state and prospects of "India, and on an elucidation at great length of "certain dogmas of the Indian philosophers."

Among the dogmas of Indian philosophers which formed the theme of conversation, was the doctrine of Absorption. There being a general desire among some of those who heard the Rajah to know more of the doctrine. Mr. Shepherd, the author of many valuable devotional works, addressed to him a letter, dated, Richmond Terrace, Clifton, Septmber 17th, 1833, in which he asked his correspondent to enlighten him and his friends of, the real opinions of those philosophic Hindus who seek absorption as the chief good. He thus stated the object of his enquiry: "I conceive it may be briefly put thus:—Do they believe that "there may be consciousnesses, or a *plurality* of "consciousness (indivisibly) in the One Total "of Happy Being?—or—Do they believe that "there can be but *one* consciousness in that One "Total of Happy Being? Only the former of "these suppositions seems to require being "illustrated. If *that* be the tenet, it appears to "me to imply that the 'Absorbed, though no "longer properly an I or *human* person, may "still someway *soliloquize*; or rather think or "utter its undivided strain in the Divine *omniloquy*, "as thus—'That which was I, but is rejoicingly "not I, exists but also fully in-exists and has its "undivided being, or in-being in the Universal "Mind. It meditates with the whole, *is* of the "whole, is blest with and in the whole. The "interposed and dissoluble which parted the "unity and continuity of the Divine *Substance*, "is gloriously removed. The substance which "was I is now not *itself* (though it exists), for "it is continuous with the whole Divine Self. "It has to will, but a mode of the universal will, "no thought but a mode of the whole thought "of the 'I am'. If such be the tenet, however "inconcieveable or dimly conceiveable (by us at "least) such a sort or modification of conscious-"ness may be, it is nevertheless not *un*conscious "being to which those philosophers aspire, but a "*mode of conscious in*existence or *in*being."

The solemn query propounded in this letter never received an answer for he to whom it was addressed was prostrated on a bed of illness from which he did not rise on this side of eternity. In the course of the conversation at Stapleton Grove, respectful enquiries concerning his religious opinions were addressed to him. To these he freely and frankly replied. After his death, which melancholy event took place soon after the Stapleton Grove party, Dr. Carpenter wrote to Mr. John Foster, the well-known Essayist, and to Dr. Jerrard, the

Principal of Bristol College, to request them to express their opinions from what they had heard in conversation with the deceased, as to whether he believed in the divinity of Christ and the resurrection and miracles. Mr. Foster replied that Rammohun Roy had expressd his belief in the resurrection of Christ, and in the Christian miracles generallay, and added " at the same time he said, " that the *internal* evidence of Christianity had " been the most decisive of his conviction. And " he gave his opinion, with some reasons for it, " that the miracles are not the part of the Christian " evidence, the best adapted to the conviction of " sceptics." Dr. Jerrard sent Dr. Carpenter the " following brief answer :—" The Rajah Ram-" mohun Roy expressed his belief in the divine " authority of Jesus Chrtst, as an accredited " messenger from God. He explicitly declared " that he believed in the miracles of Christ " generally, and particularly in his resurrection, " which he said was the foundation of the Christian " faith, and the great fact on which he rested " his own hopes of a resurrection." Mr. Estlin " the Surgeon who attended the Rajah on his " death-bed, thus jotted down in his journal :— " The Rajah said, he had denied the divinity of " Christ, but not of his commission."

This is all the evidence which Miss Carpenter adduces to prove that Rammohun Roy was a Christian. If by this it be meant that he was a thorough-going Bible-Christian, we are afraid, her position is untenable, but from a careful considera-tion of the testimony afforded by his writings, and his life, we have no hesitation in declaring our conviction that he was a Christian in the highest acceptation of the term, in as much as he tried to realize Christ in himself.

Rammohun Roy did not believe in the infallibility of the Bible. He did not believe, in the deity or divinity of Christ, but he believed that Christ was an inspired teacher of righteousness, and taught on the authority of the Most High God, and that what he taught was the Father's doctrine, not his. He regarded Christ as the greatest Reformer of the world, and the greatest soul of all the sons of men; one, before whom the majestic mind of a Vyas and a Shankaracharyya, a Kabeer and a Nanak, a Ramanand and a Chaitanaya must veil its face. He believed not that Christ was God, but that God's word was in Chirst.

Rammohun Roy might have possibly believed in the Christian miracles, but the same authority which makes this statement also assures us that he considered that "the miracles were not the part "of the Christian religion, the best adapted to the "conviction of sceptics," and "that the *internal* "evidence of Christianity had been the most "decisive of his conviction." It is, therefore, manifest that Rammohun Roy believed that the doctrines of Christianity, like the truths of Astronomy and Geology, rested not on the personal authority of the teacher, but on their own authority, on the authority of absolute truth. They rested not, in his opinion, on miracles, for if they did, Christianity would be in the same position as Hinduism, which he had denounced as a false religion. He thought that the more superstitious a nation was the stronger was the claim to miracles. The Hindus tell us that the Vedas were breathed out by Brahmá, and are a miracle; and that Vyas, the author of the Vedanta had miraculous inspiration, visions, and revelation. The Mahomedans likewise tell us that the Koran is a miracle, and that Mahomet held frequent communion with the spiritual world. In the religion of the Koles, the Khonds, and the Kanarese, all is miracle, and its authority according to miracle-mongers ought to be the best in the world. Rammohun Roy knew and felt that in resting Christianity on this basis, he would rest it on the same foundation not only with Hinduism and Mahomedanism but with the lowest form of Polytheism and Fetichism. If Rammohun Roy believed in the Christian miracles at all, he must have believed only in their possibility, not as transgressions of all law which God has made, but in their conformity with some law out of our reach. He must have regarded them as modes of divine manifestation not understood by man. Viewed in this light, life and death, mind and soul, are miracles.

We are free to confess that from his attendance at their chapels, and his known bias to their doctrines, the Unitarian Christians of England had some sort of right to claim him as a co-religionist. In the same manner the special patronage, which he thought proper to bestow on Vedantism, made it more than probable that he was a Vedantist. The laudatory terms, in which he was accustomed to speak of the doctrines of Mahomet, were calculated to produce an impression that he was a believer in the Koran. But it would be waste of time to argue that he was not a Mahomedan. Neither was he a Unitarian Christian, as the testimony of Dr Carpenter himself already quoted, proves, that while in London, although he attended the Unitarian chapels, yet *it was his system to avoid so far, identifying himself with any religious body as to make himself answerable for their acts and opinions.* We would go further and say, though it may startle and scarify the Brahmos of the old *regime'*, that he was not a Vedantist. In truth, all speculation as to his belief in any religion founded on his advocacy of certain doctrines inculcated by it, or his attendance at its place of worship are obviously futile. Rammohun Roy was essentially a Theist. He was, as we observed in the pages of this *Review* more than twenty years ago, a religious Benthamite, and estimated the different creeds existing in the world, not according to his notion of their truth, or falsehood, but by his notion of their utility; according to their tendency, in his view, to promote the maximization of human happiness, and the minimization of human misery. His patronage, therfere, of any system of creed cannot be construed into a profession of it. He endeavoured to refine all gross and idolatrous systems into a system of pure monotheism. Clear subtle, daring and deep, he aimed at revolutionizing the religious world. Endowed with the faculty of generalization and animated by an earnest desire to sift and proclaim the truth, he had critically studied the Bible, the Koran, and the Vedas. He had arrived at the conclusion that the Vedas inculcated pure monotheism, and the idolatry practised by his countrymen was a corruption of the ancient faith. He had publicly renounced that idolatry and declared it his mission to exterminate it, and to resuscitate the primitive and rational religion of the Vedas. He had learnt to appreciate the code of morality inculcated in the Bible, as the purest and loftiest; and he had done his best to expound and promulgate it to his countrymen. His three Appeals to the Christian Public, his Exposition of the Upanishads, and his Persian work *Tohufutal Mowahedeen* attest the consummate ability and unwearying zeal, with which he enforced monotheism as the substratum of the three principal religious systems of the world. His great object was to engraft a kind of universal Unitarianism on the prevailing religion of his country. But we have said that he was not a Unitarian, his Unitarianism was essentially different from that of the Channings and the Carpenters, the Priestleys and the Parkers. His was a sort of Catholic Unitarianism. It was philosophical theism. It was Natural Religion, which so many philosophers of ancient Greece and Rome followed. His advocacy and support of the cardinal doctrines inculcated by different religions, though it might apparently evince his vacillation, was in truth the result of Utilitarianism. But while he advocated the monotheistic principles of the Bible, the Vedas, and the Koran, he spared no system of idolatry. With a moral courage, rarely to be met with among Hindu reformers, he denounced the idolatrous prejudices of Hinduism, Mahomedanism, and Christianity with merciless, but impartial, severity.

This uncompromising and unsparing iconoclast while striving to eliminate superstition and hero-worship from the religious systems he had studied, failed not to extract from them the simple and saving truths of monotheism.

It has been urged by some that Rammohun Roy had no positive religious convictions whatever, but was merely a free thinker. But his whole life is an entire refutation of this charge. True he belonged to no existing sect, nor did he seek to inaugurate a new system of religion. The great ambition of his life was to promote love to God and love to men. This he tried to effect by bringing together men of existing persuasions, irrespective of all distinctions of colour and creed, into a system of universal worship of the One True and Living God. This object is indicated in unmistakable language in the Trust-Deed of the Brahmo Somaj. "The "said messuage or building, land, tenements, "hereditaments, and premises, with their appur- "tenances, to be used, occupied, enjoyed, applied "and appropriated, as and for a place of public "meeting of all sects and descriptions of people "without distinction, as shall behave and conduct "themselves in an orderly, sober, religious, and "devout manner for the worship and adoration "of the eternal, unsearchable, and immutable "Being, who is the Author and Preserver of the "universe, but not under or by any other name, "designation, or title peculiarly used for and "applied to any particular being or beings by "any man or set of men whatsoever, and that no "graven image, statue, or sculpture, carving, pain- "ting, picture, portrait, or the likeness of anything, "shall be admitted within the said messuage, "building, land, tenements, hereditaments and "premises." It is, therefore, manifest that what Rammohun Roy wanted was not unity of creed or the creation of a separate religious community like that of the Brahmos, but to spread mono-theistic worship, to establish a universal church where all classes of people,—Hindus, Mahomedans, and Christians,—would be all alike welcome to unite in the worship of their supreme and common Father. He was sincerely and unaffectedly religious. His was one of those happy and uncommon natures which could embrace all that is good in latitudinarianism, its fervent piety and its large philanthropy.

It is not our province to discuss the truth or falsity of the faith held by Rammohun Roy. We are not the apologists but the exponents of that faith. Rammohun Roy recognized no special or book-revelation. He held a record of religious truth, revealed by God to man, to be a moral impossibility. He fell back for such truth on the book of nature. He believed that the evidence of the existence and attributes of the Diety are written in the material as well as the moral world; in the frame-work and constitution of external nature, as well as in the intuitions of the human mind. He denied Original Sin and Depravity as his incisive answer to the lady already quoted shows. Though he recognized no inspired mediator or saviour, yet he believed that whenever a person with such claims has appeared, his inspiration has been the result of the beneficent impulse communicated by the Great Beneficence in proportion as the lessons He has inculacated have been wise and effective. He believed that the great business of his faith was to rest on the greatness and goodness of God. He also believed that the great First Cause of the universe is a wholly good, just, and beneficent Being, free and distinct from His works. He believed, as he himself preached, that "the Omnipotent God, "who is the only proper object of religious "veneration, is one and undivided in person;" that "in reliance on numerous promises found in "the sacred writings, we ought to entertain every "hope of enjoying the blessings of pardon from "the merciful Father, through repentance, which "is declared the only means of procuring for-"giveness for our failures;" and that "He leads "such as worship him in spirit to righteous con-"duct, and ultimately to salvation, through his "guiding influence which is called the Holy "Spirit."

We have now seen how Rammohun Roy has

stood forth in advanoe of his age and has left on it a mark which will not be easily effaced. He was the Liberator of his country from prejudice and superstition—the great Teacher from whom his countrymen were to learn to emancipate themselves from the fetters of a false religion and to worship the one true and living God. The impetus, which he communicated to the national mind is bearing it onward. Let us trust that the intellectual and moral training of the rising generation of the Hindus may land them in that position of protest against idolatry, which Rammohun Roy took as the foundation of his creed. Let us trustfully and devoutly anticipate the day, when the bitterness of sectarianism shall have ceased, and when one faith shall have brought all nations of the earth into that happy union which is in the present day the dream of many Christians, and which was certainly not one of the least fervent aspirations of Rajah Rammohun Roy.

KISSORY CHAND MITTRA.